W9-BNP-078

MY SiDEWALKS ON
SCOTT FORESMAN
READING STREET

Practice Book

Level C

PEARSON
Scott Foresman

Glenview, Illinois • Boston, Massachusetts • Chandler, Arizona
Upper Saddle River, New Jersey

ISBN-13:   978-0-328-45365-8
ISBN-10:   0-328-45365-X

12 13 14 V011 17 16 15 14

Contents

Short *a*, *i*, and *o*

Directions Read each word. Look at the letter for the vowel sound.

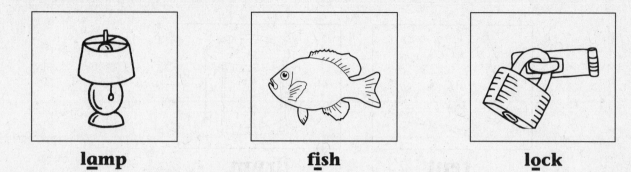

l<u>a</u>mp   f<u>i</u>sh   l<u>o</u>ck

Directions Circle the word in each sentence with the same sound as *a* in *cap*. Then write the word on the line.

_____ **1.** The cat is Rob's pet.

_____ **2.** The map is very big.

Directions Circle the word in each sentence with the same sound as *i* in *sip*. Then write the word on the line.

_____ **3.** I like to sit by the water.

_____ **4.** Their dog can do a trick.

Directions Circle the word in each sentence with the same sound as *o* in *lot*. Then write the word on the line.

_____ **5.** The sun is very hot.

_____ **6.** I found my sock!

_____ **7.** It is a very big clock.

© Pearson Education C

Home Activity This page practices words with the short *a*, *i*, and *o* sounds as in *lamp*, *fish*, and *lock*. Work through the page with your child. Have your child make a collage of magazine pictures showing items that have short *a*, *i*, and *o* sounds. Help your child label each picture.

Name_____

Short e and u

Directions Read each word. Look at the letter for the vowel sound.

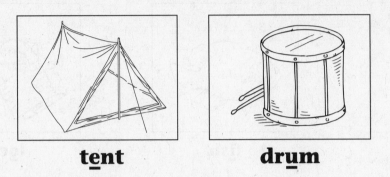

t**e**nt   dr**u**m

Directions Write two words that rhyme with each word below.

1. bet _____   _____

2. pen _____   _____

3. bump _____   _____

Directions Circle the word in each sentence with the same sound as the *e* in *then*. Then write the word on the line.

_____ **4.** We let our dog run in the park.

_____ **5.** We went to school.

_____ **6.** She got ten new hats.

Directions Circle the word in each sentence with the same sound as the *u* in *luck*. Then write the word on the line.

_____ **7.** This is such a surprise!

_____ **8.** She shut the box.

_____ **9.** The duck swam across the pond.

Home Activity This page practices the short *e* and *u* sounds as in *best* and *bump*. Work through the page with your child. Have your child write more short *e* and *u* words using the word parts *th, wh, ch,* and *ng* (*then, when, much, rung*) and use each word in a sentence.

© Pearson Education C

Name_____

Main Idea

- The **main idea** is the most important idea in a selection or a paragraph.
- The small pieces of information that tell about the main idea are the **supporting details**.

Directions Read the following passage. Then complete the Main Idea chart below.

> **D**oes your family have a pet? Cats are very good pets. They are so much fun! You will laugh when you watch them run and jump. They like to sit in your lap and let you pet them. They love it when you brush them. Cats don't have to go out when it is cold and wet. And when you are sad, they will give you a lot of love!

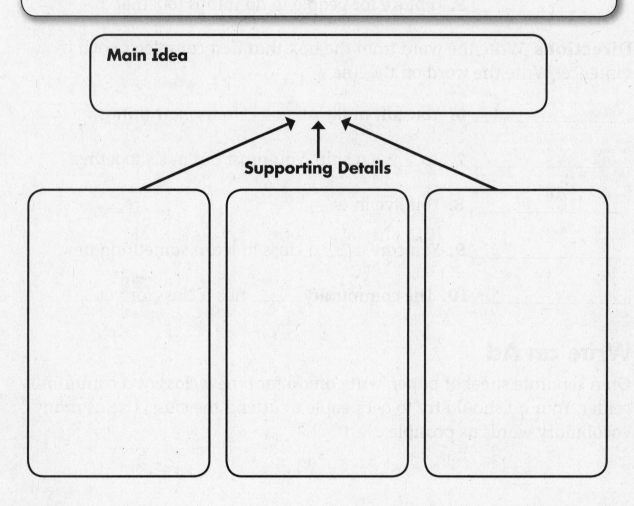

Main Idea

Supporting Details

© Pearson Education C

Home Activity This activity works with finding the main idea and supporting details. Tell your child about one of your favorite books. Ask your child to tell the main idea of what you told him or her and to identify the supporting details you gave.

Name_____

Vocabulary

Directions Choose a word from the box that best matches each definition. Write the word on the line.

_____ **1.** to put together

_____ **2.** a place where people live and work

_____ **3.** a try

_____ **4.** to be present at

_____ **5.** a place for people to do things together

Directions Write the word from the box that best completes each sentence. Write the word on the line.

_____ **6.** You can make an _____ to try new things.

_____ **7.** To _____ a ship, you must put parts together.

_____ **8.** You live in a _____ .

_____ **9.** You can _____ a class to learn something new.

_____ **10.** The community _____ has a class for you.

Write an Ad

On a separate sheet of paper, write an ad for a new class at a community center. Your ad should try to get people to attend the class. Use as many vocabulary words as possible.

© Pearson Education C

Home Activity This page helps your child learn to read and write the words *attend, build, center, community,* and *effort*. Work through the items with your child. Then ask your child to write the words and read them aloud.

Name_____

Writing

Directions Choose an activity that you could try. You can use an idea from the box or another one you like better. Write about your activity on the lines.

| build something | learn to drum | get in a bug club |
| learn to sing | attend a camp | take an acting class |

1. I could _____

_____ .

2. Where could you do this?

I could _____

_____ .

3. Why do you want to try this?

_____

4. What part could be the most fun?

_____

5. What part could take the most effort?

_____

Use your answers and other ideas to write several sentences about trying something new.

_____

_____

_____

© Pearson Education C

School + Home **Home Activity** This page helps your child think of how to complete a writing assignment about trying new things. Work through the page with your child. Then discuss your child's answers.

Long Vowels CVCe

Directions Add an *e* to the end of each word to make a new word. Write the new word on the line.

_____ **1.** tub   _____ **4.** can

_____ **2.** slid   _____ **5.** hop

_____ **3.** pet

Directions Circle the words that have the same vowel sound as the picture name.

plane	take	tack	game	whale	lake
	chase	grape	cap	trade	sad

rose	bone	lot	note	job	code
	joke	home	book	stone	wrote

mice	ride	five	skip	white	kite
	lick	like	tribe	ring	bike

flute	cute	use	bus	much	tube
	mule	gum	fun	cube	drum

Home Activity This page practices words with long vowel sounds in words such as *grade, these, kite, bone,* and *cute*. Work through the page with your child. Challenge your child to use each of the new words from items 1–5 in sentences. Have him or her identify the long vowel sound in each word.

© Pearson Education C

Name_____

c/s/, g/j/, and s/z/

Directions Circle the word that names the picture.

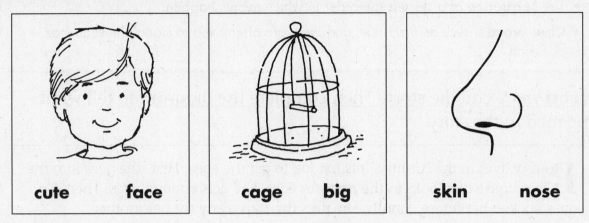

| cute   face | cage   big | skin   nose |

Directions Circle the words that have a sound like the *c* in *face*.

| race | nice | cat | rice | come |

| place | tick | cent | lace | fence |

Directions Circle the words that have a sound like the *g* in *gem*.

| orange | goat | gum | page | thing |

| age | ago | stage | huge | good |

Directions Circle the words that have a sound like the *s* in *use*.

| rose | past | same | hose | those |

| these | said | chose | his | wish |

Home Activity This page practices words that have the /s/ sound spelled *c* as in *race*, the /j/ sound spelled *g* as in *cage*, and the /z/ sound spelled *s* as in *rose*. Work through the page with your child. Have your child complete this sentence by changing the underscored items: *Face* is spelled with a <u>c</u> but it has the sound of an <u>s</u>.

Name_____

Sequence

- The **sequence** of a story is the order in which events happen.
- **Clue words**, such as *first*, *next*, and *then*, are often used to signal the sequence of events.

Directions Read the story. Then complete the diagram to tell what happened in the story.

> Penny lives in the country. It is her job to get the eggs. First, she goes into the hen house and looks in the nests for eggs. She gets enough eggs. Then she goes back to her house. Finally, she puts the eggs away for her mother.

Title_____

```
┌──────────────────────────────────────────────┐
│ 1. Beginning                                   │
│                                                │
│                                                │
└──────────────────────────────────────────────┘
                       │
                       ▼
┌──────────────────────────────────────────────┐
│ 2. Middle                                      │
│                                                │
│                                                │
└──────────────────────────────────────────────┘
                       │
                       ▼
┌──────────────────────────────────────────────┐
│ 3. End                                         │
│                                                │
│                                                │
└──────────────────────────────────────────────┘
```

4. Circle clue words in the story that tell the order of events. Then write them on the line below.

_____

Home Activity This page works with the order of events in a story. Work through the page together. Then have your child retell the story while acting out what happens.

© Pearson Education C

Name_____

Vocabulary

Directions Match each word with its definition. Write the word on the line.

_____ 1. the stuff used to buy things

_____ 2. give something and get something

_____ 3. things to buy

_____ 4. what one thinks is its price

_____ 5. another word for trade

Directions Write a word from the box to complete each sentence below.

6. Tom had some _____ to buy a bike.

7. The new bike was _____ a lot of money.

8. First, he wanted to _____ his old bike for the new one.

9. Then he thought he would _____ several things with his friends.

10. Finally, Tom said he did not want to buy any of the _____ .

Make a Poster

Imagine that your class is going to have a trade fair or a swap meet. Make a poster telling about it. Use as many of the vocabulary words as you can.

Home Activity This page helps your child learn to read and write the words *goods, money, swap, trade,* and *worth*. Work through the items with your child. Then ask your child to write the words and read them aloud.

Practice Book Unit 1

Vocabulary 9

© Pearson Education C

Name_____

Writing

Directions Think about a trade you would like to make. Then follow the steps below.

Step 1 Make a list of things you have to trade.

_____   _____
_____   _____
_____   _____

Step 2 Make a list of things you want to trade for.

_____   _____
_____   _____
_____   _____

Step 3 Make a list of people you might trade with.

_____   _____
_____   _____
_____   _____

Step 4 Go back to Step 1 and circle the thing you will trade.

Step 5 Go back to Step 2 and circle the thing you will trade for.

Step 6 Go back to Step 3 and circle the name of the person you will trade with.

On another sheet of paper, use your answers to write about a trade you would like to make. Be sure to tell why you want to trade.

School + Home **Home Activity** This page helps your child plan to write about a trade. Work through the page with your child. When your child finishes writing about a trade, listen to your child read the paragraph aloud.

Name_____

Plurals and Inflected Endings -s, -es

Directions Add **-s** to each word. Write the new word on the line.

1. cat _____

2. send _____

3. ship _____

4. frog _____

5. bump _____

6. bake _____

7. clam _____

8. code _____

9. cube _____

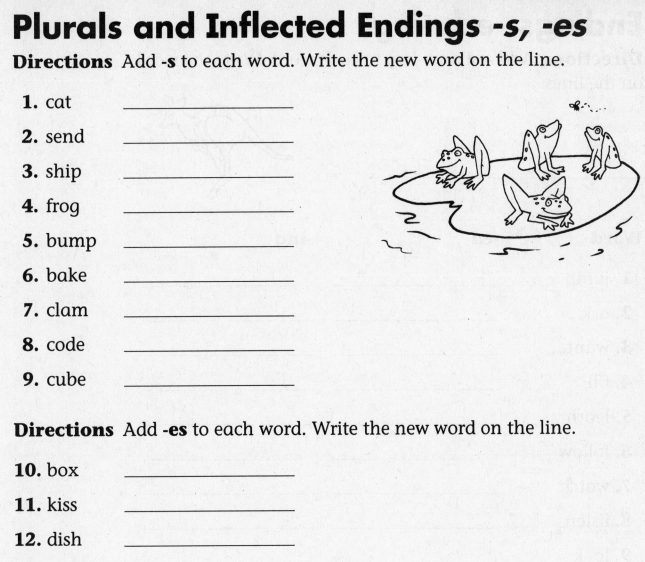

Directions Add **-es** to each word. Write the new word on the line.

10. box _____

11. kiss _____

12. dish _____

13. catch _____

14. punch _____

15. brush _____

Home Activity This page practices adding -s and -es to the end of words. Work through the items with your child. Write these words: *color, wish, word, glass.* Ask your child to add -s or -es to show more than one.

Name_____

Endings -ed, -ing

Directions Add **-ed** and **-ing** to each word. Write the words on the lines.

Word	-ed	-ing
1. jump	_____	_____
2. ask	_____	_____
3. want	_____	_____
4. fill	_____	_____
5. learn	_____	_____
6. follow	_____	_____
7. watch	_____	_____
8. listen	_____	_____
9. look	_____	_____
10. push	_____	_____
11. work	_____	_____
12. pull	_____	_____
13. laugh	_____	_____
14. wash	_____	_____
15. remember	_____	_____

© Pearson Education C

Home Activity This page practices words with the endings *-ed* and *-ing*. Work through the items with your child. Write these words: *touch, cover, spill, print.* Ask your child to add *-ed* and *-ing* to each word and then say the new words.

Name_____

Sequence

- **Sequence** is the order in which events happen in a story.
- Look for these **clue words**: *first, next, then, finally.*
- As you read, **think about** what happens. This will help you keep track of the sequence of events.

Directions Read the passage.

Jim loves to draw pictures of a place in the country. First, he draws some grass in a big field. Next, he makes a big old house.

He makes a sun in the sky and colors it yellow. Then he draws some people and animals. Finally, he colors everything in the picture.

Directions Use the diagram to tell about the events of the story in the correct order.

First

↓

Next

↓

Then

↓

Finally

© Pearson Education C

Home Activity This page allows your child to identify the sequence of events in a story. Name four events that happened in your family during the last year. Do not tell them in the order they happened. Ask your child to put them in the correct order. Encourage your child to use the words *first, next, then,* and *finally.*

Name_____

Vocabulary

Directions Draw a line from the word to its definition.

> ### Check the Words You Know
>
> __allowance   __expensive
> __amount   __savings
> __deposit

1. deposit   at a very big price

2. amount   something put in a place to be kept safe

3. allowance   a sum of money given to someone

4. savings   the sum

5. expensive   money saved

Directions Choose a word from the box that fits the meaning of the sentence. Write the word on the line.

6. Ali gets money for her _____ .

7. She puts some of the money in the bank as _____ .

8. The money she puts in the bank is a _____ .

9. Ali hopes to save a big _____ soon.

10. She wants to buy an _____ game.

Write a Description

What could you do to earn money? On a separate paper, name some things you could do. Then tell which you would like best and why. Write at least three sentences. Use as many vocabulary words as you can.

School + Home   **Home Activity** This page helps your child read and write vocabulary words. Work through the items with your child. Then ask your child to read his or her description aloud.

© Pearson Education C

Name_____

Writing

Think about something you could save for. It should not be too expensive. Think about how you can get money and how much of it you can save.

Directions Finish the sentences below.

1. I want to save to buy a _____ .

2. My allowance is $_____ .

3. I can save $_____ from my allowance.

4. I can get money by

_____

_____

_____

5. I think it will take _____ to save enough money.

6. Write a good first sentence. Tell what you want to buy.

_____

7. Write a good second sentence. Tell why you want it.

_____

On a separate paper, write about what you would buy and why. Be sure to tell how you would save enough money. Use the sentences you completed above to help you. Make sure all your words are spelled correctly.

© Pearson Education C

Home Activity This page helps your child write about a topic. Work through the page with your child. Then have your child read the sentences aloud.

Base Words and Endings -ed, -ing

Directions Add **-ed** and **-ing** to each word and write the new words. Remember to double the last consonant.

Word	-ed	-ing
1. stop	_____	_____
2. skim	_____	_____
3. drop	_____	_____
4. swap	_____	_____
5. plan	_____	_____
6. grab	_____	_____
7. shop	_____	_____
8. hop	_____	_____
9. tug	_____	_____
10. beg	_____	_____
11. fill	_____	_____
12. hug	_____	_____

 Home Activity This page practices adding *-ed* and *-ing* to words. Work through the items with your child. Read a story with your child. Help him or her find words ending in *-ed* and *-ing* that double the last consonant before adding the ending.

Base Words and Endings -ed, -ing

Directions Add **-ed** and **-ing** to each word and write the new words.
Remember to drop the final **e**.

Word	-ed	-ing
1. race	_____	_____
2. hope	_____	_____
3. wipe	_____	_____
4. chase	_____	_____
5. blame	_____	_____
6. trade	_____	_____
7. change	_____	_____
8. believe	_____	_____
9. like	_____	_____
10. use	_____	_____
11. move	_____	_____
12. promise	_____	_____

© Pearson Education C

Home Activity This page practices adding *-ed* and *-ing* to words. Work through the items with your child. Read a story with your child. Help him or her find words ending in *-ed* and *-ing* that follow the rule on this page.

Compare and Contrast

- When you **compare** and **contrast**, you tell how two or more things are alike and different.

Directions Read the story. Then answer the questions below.

Teddy and Freddy are animals. They work and have fun. It is hot, and they need to make plans for the time when it gets cold. When it is cold, they can't find things to eat. They must find it now and save it.

Freddy looks for nuts. He puts them in a safe place. Then he goes to see his friends. Teddy looks for fun things to do. He spends a few minutes finding nuts. Freddy tells him to work. But Teddy doesn't listen. He likes to have fun!

When it is cold, Freddy has lots of nuts to eat. He is full. Teddy has nothing to eat. He has to ask Freddy to lend him something to eat. He promises to help next time.

How are Teddy and Freddy alike?

1. They are _____ .

2. They _____ and have _____ .

3. They must find _____ to eat and _____ it for the winter.

How are Teddy and Freddy different?

4. Freddy _____ for nuts, but Teddy just has _____ .

5. When it is cold, Freddy has _____ to eat, but Teddy has _____ .

6. Think of words to contrast Teddy and Freddy. Freddy _____ , but Teddy _____ .

© Pearson Education C

School + Home **Home Activity** This page helps your child compare and contrast. Work through the items with your child. Read an animal story or fable with your child. Ask him or her to compare and contrast two characters.

Name_____

Vocabulary

Directions Solve each riddle with a word from the box. Write the word on the line.

Check the Words You Know

___coin
___dollar
___nickel
___penny
___quarter

1. I am 1¢.

What am I? _____

2. I am 25¢.

What am I? _____

3. I am 100 cents.

What am I? _____

4. I am 5 pennies.

What am I? _____

5. I am a round piece of money.

What am I? _____

Directions Write the word from the box that fits the sentence on the line.

6. I used the _____ to get the 5 cent picture.

7. I used the _____ to get the 25 cent box.

8. I used the _____ to get the 100 cent cap.

9. I used the _____ to get the 1 cent surprise.

10. A penny is a _____ .

Write a Story

Imagine that you have a coin collection. Write a story about your coins. Use as many vocabulary words as possible to describe the collection.

© Pearson Education C

Home Activity This page helps your child read and write vocabulary words. Work through the items with your child. Then ask your child to read his or her story to you.

Name_____

Writing

Directions Think about things people want or need. Look at the words in the box for ideas. Then answer the questions.

1. What are some things people need? List them.

_____   _____

_____   _____

water
socks
a kite
a picture
things to eat
a game
a place to live
a bat

2. What are some things people want? List them.

_____   _____

_____   _____

3. Where can you get these things?

_____

_____

4. How can you get money to get these things?

_____

_____

On another paper, draw a coin or a bill. Draw the front and back. Then write about your money. Tell its name and how much it is. Tell if you will use the money to get a want or a need.

© Pearson Education C

School + Home **Home Activity** This page helps your child write about wants and needs. Work through the page with your child. Ask your child to show you the picture and read the description aloud.

20 Writing   **Practice Book Unit 1**

Syllables VC/CV

Directions Circle the words in the box with a **short vowel** sound in **the first syllable.** Write the words on the lines.

afraid	become	fossil	intend	object	today
always	easy	happen	invent	people	zigzag

1. _____

2. _____

3. _____

4. _____

5. _____

6. _____

Directions Choose a word from the box to complete each sentence. Write the word on the line.

ribbon	lesson	mitten	rabbit

_____ **7.** Ed's pet _____ is little.

_____ **8.** Mary lost her _____ on the ice.

_____ **9.** The box had a _____ on it.

_____ **10.** Today's _____ at school was about snakes.

Home Activity This page practices words with short vowels in the first syllable. Work through the items with your child. Ask your child to write sentences about a kitten who went on a picnic.

© Pearson Education C

Name_____

Syllables VC/CV

Directions Circle each word that has a **short vowel** sound in the first syllable and a **long vowel** sound in the last syllable. Write the word on the line.

_____ 1. A tadpole becomes a frog.

_____ 2. A snake is a reptile.

_____ 3. I have a trombone for the school band.

_____ 4. You inhale through your nose.

_____ 5. I made one mistake on the math test.

Directions Circle the word in each row that has a **short vowel** sound in the first syllable and a **long vowel** sound in the last syllable.

6. umpire	boxes	promise
7. cover	exhale	minute
8. admire	question	color
9. woman	because	engage
10. either	stepping	invite

© Pearson Education C

Home Activity This page practices words with short vowels and long vowels. Work through the items with your child. Ask your child to tell what letter stands for the short vowel sound in the words *tadpole* and *reptile*.

Name_____

Draw Conclusions

- A **conclusion** is a decision you make after you think about details and facts.
- Think about **what you already know** to draw a conclusion.

Directions Read the three details in the boxes. Then write a conclusion—what you think will happen.

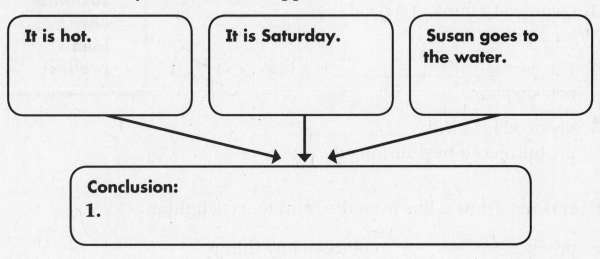

| It is hot. | It is Saturday. | Susan goes to the water. |

Conclusion:
1.

Directions Read the conclusion. Then write one more detail that will help someone draw that conclusion.

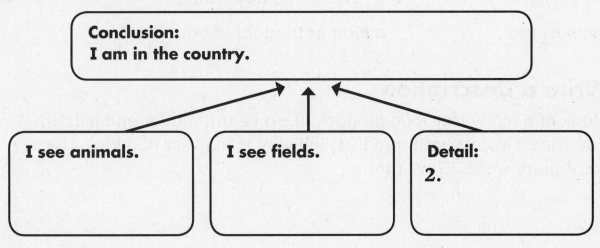

Conclusion:
I am in the country.

| I see animals. | I see fields. | Detail:
2. |

Home Activity This page helps your child use details to draw a conclusion. Work through the items with your child. Read a story with your child. Stop now and then and ask your child to draw a conclusion about one of the characters.

Vocabulary

Directions Fill in the blank with a word from the box that fits the meaning of the sentence.

1. The _____ sells things for pets.

2. One _____ wants a gift for a dog.

3. I wanted to think of a good _____ for a gift.

4. The best _____ is a big new dog bone.

5. My good idea will _____ the business a new customer!

> ### Check the Words You Know
> __business
> __customer
> __earn
> __idea
> __product

Directions Draw a line from the word to its definition.

6. product   a place to buy things

7. idea   to get money for work

8. earn   something that is made

9. customer   a person who buys things

10. business   a plan or thought in your head

Write a Description

Think of a really icky food product, like a peanut butter and jellyfish sandwich. Describe your product. Tell why it is a very bad idea. Use vocabulary words. Have fun!

© Pearson Education C.

Home Activity This page helps your child read and write vocabulary words. Work through the items with your child. Help your child think of other unusual food products and tell about the product and the business that would sell it.

Name_____

Writing

Directions Use the web below to list product ideas. Tell why they are good ideas. They can be serious—a cat box that cleans itself. Or they can be silly—magic soap you use one time and never have to take a bath again. You can put different topics in the web if you like.

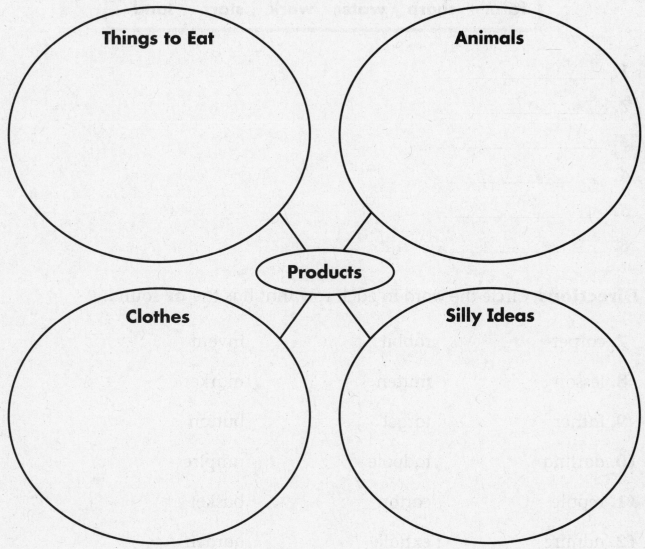

Write a Description

On separate paper, list your ten best ideas. Draw a star by the very best idea. Describe the product and tell why it is a good idea. Tell who would buy it. Be sure all your words are spelled correctly.

School + Home
Home Activity This page helps your child describe a product. Work through the page with your child. Ask your child to tell you about his or her second-best product idea.

© Pearson Education C

r-Controlled *ar*

Directions Circle the words in the box that have the sound **ar**.
Write the words on the lines.

yarn	art	barn	ever	here	hour
farm	sharp	water	work	star	land

1. _____

2. _____

3. _____

4. _____

5. _____

6. _____

Directions Circle the word in each row that has the **ar** sound.

7. carpet   rabbit   invent

8. lesson   mitten   market

9. father   target   button

10. darling   tadpole   umpire

11. reptile   carton   basket

12. admire   exhale   garden

Home Activity This page practices words with *ar*. Work through the items with your child. Ask your child to name something in your home that is large, something that is sharp, and something someone bought at a market.

© Pearson Education C

Name_____

r-Controlled *or, ore*

Directions Circle the word in each sentence that has **or** or **ore**.
Write the word on the line.

_____ **1.** I want to build a fort on a hill.

_____ **2.** Peg was born in June.

_____ **3.** Can I have some more water?

_____ **4.** We buy things to eat at the store.

_____ **5.** It is cold at the North Pole.

_____ **6.** We are eating corn.

_____ **7.** Leo likes to play sports.

_____ **8.** Bill can ride a horse.

Directions Underline the word in ( ) that has **or** or **ore**.
Then write the word on the line.

_____ **9.** We like to eat (apples, popcorn) at the movies.

_____ **10.** Janet lives around the (block, corner) from me.

_____ **11.** When you count, 1 comes (after, before) 2.

_____ **12.** We like to (explore, play) in the park.

© Pearson Education C

Home Activity This page practices words with *or* and *ore*. Work through the items with your child. Ask your child to make up a silly sentence that uses these words: *corn, fork, horse.*

Main Idea

- The **main idea** is what a story is all about.
- **Details** are small facts that help tell what the story is about.

Directions Read the story. Then answer the questions.

Two pigs wanted to eat corn. They planted some seeds. They both watered the plants and watched the plants get bigger. They picked the corn together too.

"We have too much corn," said Peter Pig.

"We can give some corn to our friends," said Harry Hog.

Their friends were thrilled. "You are smart farmers," said Cindy Cow. "You are very nice," said Sally Sheep. "You are good friends," said Gus Goat.

After that, Peter and Harry planted corn every spring. When they picked the corn, they always gave some to their friends.

1. Circle the sentence that tells what the story is about.

> **Main Idea**
> Animals like to eat corn.
> Two pigs give corn to their friends.
> Corn needs water to get bigger.

Write details that help tell about the main idea.

Detail	**Detail**	**Detail**
2. Cindy Cow said:	**3.** Sally Sheep said:	**4.** Gus Goat said:

Home Activity This page helps your child find the main idea and details in a story. Work through the items with your child. Ask your child to tell you about the lesson he or she learned from the story.

Name_____

Vocabulary

Directions Draw a line from the word to
its definition.

1. environment   to save from harm or danger

2. adapt   to live through hard times

3. wildlife   everything that is around you

4. protect   wild animals and plants

5. survive   to change to fit different things

Directions Fill in the blank with the word from the box that fits the
meaning of the sentence.

6. Some animals live in a cold _____ .

7. A fish cannot _____ out of water.

8. Rabbits are _____ that live in the country fields.

9. Mother animals work to _____ their young.

10. A big snake cannot change, or _____ , to
become a good pet.

Write an Advertisement

Choose an animal. Imagine that you are that animal. On a separate
paper, write an ad about you! Tell why people should come see you at the
zoo. Try to use vocabulary words.

© Pearson Education C

Name_____

Writing

Directions Plan what you will do. The questions below will help you. Write your ideas on the lines.

1. Choose an environment. It could be a hot, dry place; a cold place like the North Pole; or another place.

   _____

2. What animals will you show?

   _____ _____ _____

   _____ _____ _____

3. What outdoor things are in the environment? Think about grass, plants, and water.

   _____ _____ _____

   _____ _____ _____

4. How will you tell about your place on a poster?

   _____

5. How will you draw the environment? You can use crayons, markers, or paint. You also can cut out magazine pictures and put them on your poster.

   _____

Make a Poster

Use a large sheet of paper to make a big poster. Draw your animals in their environment. Write sentences to tell how they adapt. Be sure your words are spelled correctly.

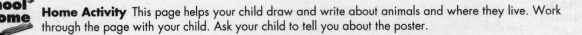

School + Home **Home Activity** This page helps your child draw and write about animals and where they live. Work through the page with your child. Ask your child to tell you about the poster.

© Pearson Education C

Name_____

Possessives

Directions Circle the possessive word in each sentence. Write the word on the line.

_____ **1.** The frog's skin is green.

_____ **2.** My sister's name is Beth.

_____ **3.** The kids' room was a mess.

_____ **4.** Our brother's birthday is today.

_____ **5.** The robins' nests are in trees.

_____ **6.** Fred's cap is red and green.

_____ **7.** The Earth's water is blue.

_____ **8.** Don't take my dog's bone!

_____ **9.** I looked at my friend's picture.

_____ **10.** My mom's cake smells good.

_____ **11.** I will toss a stick to Gus's dog.

_____ **12.** My father's idea was good.

_____ **13.** My neighbors' cats are very large.

_____ **14.** Our family's name is Miller.

_____ **15.** The house's steps are wet.

© Pearson Education C

School + Home **Home Activity** This page practices possessive words. Work through the items with your child. Read a story with your child. Ask him or her to point to words that are possessives.

Name_____

r-Controlled *er, ir, ur*

Directions Underline the word in each sentence with the sound **er** spelled **er**. Write the word on the line.

_____ **1.** A germ can make you sick.

_____ **2.** Do you know her name?

_____ **3.** Ken can whisper.

_____ **4.** The house is made of lumber.

_____ **5.** That book has a robot on the cover.

Directions Underline the word in each sentence with the sound **er** spelled **ir**. Write the word on the line.

_____ **6.** Tim is in first grade.

_____ **7.** I am in third grade.

_____ **8.** Mom twirls when we dance.

_____ **9.** This girl is my best friend.

_____ **10.** We sat in a tent at the circus.

Directions Underline the word in each sentence with the sound **er** spelled **ur**. Write the word on the line.

_____ **11.** It is my turn to tell a joke.

_____ **12.** The pig's tail has a curl.

_____ **13.** I like to swim in the surf.

_____ **14.** Fish can survive in the lake.

Home Activity This page practices words with the vowel sound er spelled er, ir, and ur. Work through the items with your child. Write this sentence and read it to your child: *You better not get butter on your mother's sweater.* Ask your child to say the words with the sound er.

© Pearson Education C

Name_____

Compare and Contrast

- When you **compare and contrast,** you tell how things are alike and different.
- You can use a **Venn diagram** to help you **compare and contrast.**

Directions Read the passage.

Frogs and fish are a lot alike, but they are not the same.

Frogs and fish can swim in the water. Both frogs and fish eat other animals. Both can be green.

Frogs live in the water and on land. Fish can live only in water.

Frogs have legs. They use legs to jump and swim. Fish have fins. They use their fins to swim.

Directions Finish the Venn diagram to compare and contrast frogs and fish. On the left side, tell things about frogs. On the right side, tell things about fish. In the middle, tell things that are the same about frogs and fish.

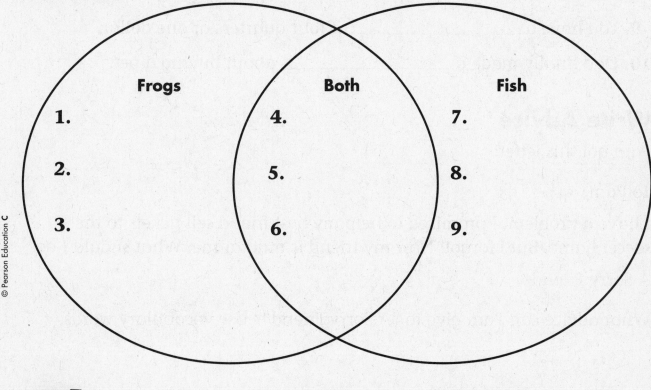

Frogs

1.

2.

3.

Both

4.

5.

6.

Fish

7.

8.

9.

Home Activity This page helps your child compare and contrast. Work through the items with your child. Then ask your child to compare and contrast two people in your family.

Name_____

Vocabulary

Directions Draw a line from the word to its definition.

1. advice   the act of deciding

2. decide   words about what should be done

3. problem   a hard question

4. decision   something picked out

5. choice   to choose something

Directions Fill in the blank with the word from the box that fits the meaning of the sentence.

6. You can _____ to write a long letter or a short note.

7. It is a _____ if your bike has a flat tire.

8. "Do not tell a lie" is good _____ .

9. You have a _____ of four quarters or one dollar.

10. Dad finally made a _____ about buying a pet.

Write Advice

Pam got this letter:

To Pam,

I have a problem. I promised to help my best friend sell tickets to the soccer game. But I forgot! Now my friend is mad at me. What should I do?

A Sorry Friend

What advice can Pam give to "A Sorry Friend"? Use vocabulary words.

© Pearson Education C

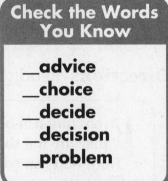

School + Home **Home Activity** This page helps your child read and write vocabulary words. Work through the items with your child. Then ask your child to read you his or her advice aloud.

Name_____

Writing

Directions Not all decisions are easy to make. You must be brave to make some decisions. Read each question. Write your answers on the lines.

1. How was Rosa Parks brave?

_____

_____

2. Do you think she was sorry that she did not get up for the man?

_____

3. What happened because of Rosa Parks's decision?

_____

_____

4. Was Curt brave when he did not invite Gertrude to his party?

_____

_____

5. Was Curt brave when he invited Gertrude?

_____

_____

6. Write sentences that tell about Rosa Parks and Curt.

Rosa Parks was brave because _____.

Curt was brave because _____.

On another paper, tell about how Rosa Parks and Curt were brave. Tell about their choices and how they felt later. Use vocabulary words. Check your spelling.

© Pearson Education C

School + Home **Home Activity** This page helps your child write about decisions people make. Work through the page with your child. Then ask your child to tell about a time when it was not easy for him or her to make a decision.

Name_____

Endings -er, -est

Directions Add **-er** and **-est** to each word. Remember that you may have to double the last consonant. Write the words on the lines.

Word	-er	-est
1. soft	_____	_____
2. short	_____	_____
3. wild	_____	_____
4. new	_____	_____
5. warm	_____	_____
6. kind	_____	_____
7. soon	_____	_____
8. full	_____	_____
9. poor	_____	_____
10. young	_____	_____
11. cold	_____	_____
12. long	_____	_____
13. old	_____	_____
14. big	_____	_____
15. sad	_____	_____

Home Activity This page practices words with the endings -er and -est. Work through the items with your child. Line up sets of three things that are different heights or lengths. Ask your child to say which item is big/bigger/biggest and long/longer/longest.

© Pearson Education C

Name_____

Vowel Sounds of y

Directions Choose the word in ( ) with the **long i** sound for **y**.
Write the word on the line.

_____ **1.** Jane is (my, may) name.

_____ **2.** Our house is (boy, by) the park.

_____ **3.** I (cry, city) when I get hurt.

_____ **4.** Birds like to (fire, fly).

_____ **5.** We (try, toy) to spell all the words.

Directions Circle the words in the box with the **long e** sound for **y**.
Write the words on the lines.

away	buy	carry	enjoy	funny	happy
pretty	silly	sorry	today	penny	

6. _____   **10.** _____

7. _____   **11.** _____

8. _____   **12.** _____

9. _____

School + Home **Home Activity** This page practices words with the long *i* and long *e* sounds of *y*. Work through the items with your child. Ask your child to write a sentence that uses the word *try* and tells something he or she would like to do.

Name_____

Main Idea

- The **main idea** is what a story is all about.
- **Details** are small pieces of information about the main idea.

Directions Read the story. Then answer the questions.

"Oh, no!" said Lin. "Today is Mom's party. I forgot to buy her a card."

Lin decided to make a card. She wanted it to be special. She thought for a long time. Then she had an idea.

Lin took some red paper. In pencil, she wrote I LOVE YOU MOM! Then she got Mom's button box.

She used paste to put the buttons over her pencil lines.

Oh, no! All the buttons are gone, and MOM! is still in pencil.

Lin had another idea. She got peas from the kitchen. She used paste to put the peas over the last pencil lines.

Lin's mom said she loved the birthday card.

What is the main idea of the story? Write it in the box. Write three details that tell about the main idea.

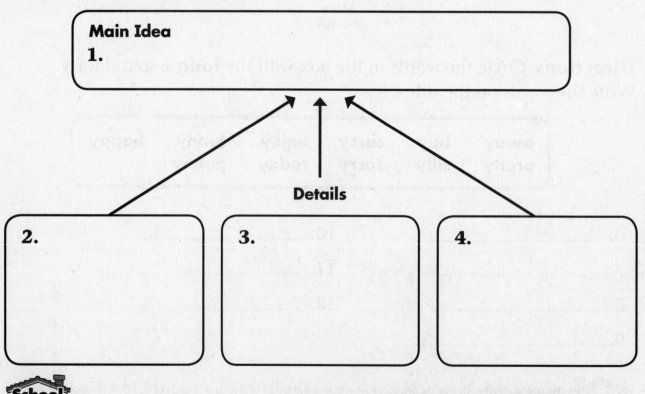

Main Idea
1.

Details

2.

3.

4.

© Pearson Education C

School + Home **Home Activity** This page helps your child practice finding the main idea and details in a story. Work through the items with your child. Ask your child if he or she thinks that Lin's ideas were good.

Name_____

Vocabulary

Directions Choose the vocabulary word from the box and write it next to its meaning.

_____ 1. to not do something

_____ 2. the answer to a problem

_____ 3. to find the answer

_____ 4. a game with many small parts

_____ 5. a new thing that someone makes

Directions Each sentence has a word missing. Circle the word at the end of each sentence that fits the meaning. Then write the word on the line.

6. Can you _____ this problem for me? solve fail

7. The _____ is the answer. puzzle solution

8. Film is a good _____ . invention solve

9. This _____ has too many parts! puzzle solve

10. My idea for a robot will not _____ . invention fail

What Do You Think?

Tad invented a machine that can wash a dog alone. You put your dog in the machine, and it washes the dog in five minutes. You do nothing! Write a review of Tad's invention. Tell if you think it is a good idea or a bad idea. Use as many vocabulary words as you can.

© Pearson Education C

Home Activity This page helps your child read and write vocabulary words. Work through the items with your child. Ask your child to read his or her review out loud to you.

Name_____

Writing

Directions With your partner, talk about problems that could be solved with inventions. List some of them here.

_____

_____

_____

Talk about how you could solve the problems. Choose a problem and write it in the Problem box. Then write ideas for how to solve it in the Solution box. Think of an invention.

Problem

↓

Solution

Use another paper to draw a picture of an invention. Use pencil first. Then go over your lines with color pencils or markers. Write sentences to tell about your invention. Check the spelling of all your words.

School + Home

Home Activity This page helps your child describe a problem and a solution. Work through the page with your child. Then have your child read aloud his or her sentences about the invention.

Name_____

Base Words and Endings
-es, -ed, -er, -est

Directions Add **-es** and **-ed** to each word. Remember to change **y** to **i**.
Write the words on the lines.

Word	**-es**	**-ed**
1. try	_____	_____
2. cry	_____	_____
3. dry	_____	_____
4. worry	_____	_____
5. carry	_____	_____

Directions Add **-er** and **-est** to each word. Remember to change **y** to **i**.
Write the words on the lines.

Word	**-er**	**-est**
6. funny	_____	_____
7. happy	_____	_____
8. muddy	_____	_____
9. early	_____	_____
10. heavy	_____	_____

© Pearson Education C

School + Home **Home Activity** This page practices words that end with *-es*, *-ed*, *-er*, and *-est*. Work through the items with your child. Write *bunny*, *puppy*, and *party*. Ask your child to add *-es* to each word and to write the new words.

Consonant Blends

Directions Underline the consonant blend at the beginning or the end of each word. Then write the word on the line.

1. smile _____

2. jump _____

3. first _____

4. stripe _____

5. mint _____

6. strip _____

7. bring _____

Directions Choose the word in ( ) with a consonant blend to complete each sentence. Write the word on the line.

_____ **8.** I like to (splash, sit) in the lake.

_____ **9.** We read a story about (nice, three) bears.

_____ **10.** Can you (stretch, move) your arm up?

_____ **11.** You must be (tired, strong) to carry me!

_____ **12.** (Scrub, Put) your legs in the bath.

Home Activity This page practices words with consonant blends, such as *strip, smile, splash, jump,* and *scrub.* Work through the items with your child. Ask your child to say and write five words that end in *nd.*

© Pearson Education C

Name_____

Sequence

- **Sequence** is the order in which things happen in a story.
- Look for **clue words** such as *first*, *second*, *next*, *then*, and *last*.

Directions Read the story.

Liz's dog Buster ran in the mud. He was very dirty. He needed a bath.

First, Liz got a big tub and the hose. Liz filled the tub with water. She got Buster's towel.

Next, Liz called for Buster. But he would not come. Buster hates baths! Liz found Buster under her bed. She pulled Buster and made him get in the tub.

Then Liz washed Buster all over. When the bath was finished, Buster started to shake himself dry—and Liz got all wet!

Last, Liz had to get dry. Buster did not use the towel. Instead, Liz used Buster's towel.

Directions Write these sentences in the correct place on the chart.

- Buster hid under the bed.
- Liz got a big tub and a hose.

- Liz used Buster's towel.
- Liz washed Buster.

First
1.

Next
2.

Then
3.

Last
4.

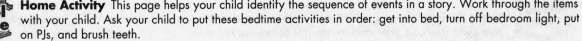

School + Home **Home Activity** This page helps your child identify the sequence of events in a story. Work through the items with your child. Ask your child to put these bedtime activities in order: get into bed, turn off bedroom light, put on PJs, and brush teeth.

Name_____

Vocabulary

Directions Draw a line to match each word with
a meaning for that word.

1. responsible   having pride in what you do

2. right   not right; bad

3. proud   something you must do

4. responsibility   good and correct

5. wrong   being in charge

**Check the Words
You Know**

__proud
__responsibility
__responsible
__right
__wrong

Directions Write the word from the box that best completes
each sentence.

_____ 6. Taking care of a pet is a big _____ .

_____ 7. It is _____ to hit another person.

_____ 8. Tim was _____ when he won the race.

_____ 9. Saying "please" and "thank you" are the _____
things to do.

_____ 10. Who is _____ for getting the papers?

Write a Story

Imagine that a student *did* take pet mice to school. On another paper,
write about what happened. Use as many vocabulary words as you can.

Home Activity This page helps your child read and write vocabulary words. Work through the items with
your child. Then ask your child to read his or her story to you.

© Pearson Education C

Name_____

Writing

Some people are **not** responsible:

- They break promises.
- They make a mistake and don't admit it. Or they blame another person.
- They do not watch what they do.
- They do wrong things.

Directions Think about what a child would be like if he or she were **not** responsible. Write your answers to the questions below.

1. What are some things he or she would do?

_____   _____

_____   _____

2. What would happen because he or she was not responsible? For example, what would happen if the child spilled milk or did not give the dog water?

_____

_____

_____

3. How would the child's family feel? How would his or her friends feel?

_____

_____

4. How would the child feel about not being responsible?

_____

_____

On another paper, write a story about a character who is not responsible. Use as many vocabulary words as you can. Check the spelling of all your words.

School + Home **Home Activity** This page helps your child write a story. Work through the page with your child. Ask your child if he or she is responsible or is not responsible. Then have your child read his or her story to you.

Name_____

Syllables VC/V and V/CV

Directions Circle the words in the box with a **short vowel** sound in the **first syllable.** Then write the words on the lines.

robot	body	comet	finish	frozen
never	notice	over	hotel	travel

1. _____

2. _____

3. _____

4. _____

5. _____

Directions Circle the words in the box with a **long vowel** sound in the **first syllable.** Then use the words to complete the sentences. Write each word on the line.

baby	comic	even	ever	lemon
spider	minute	zebra	panel	pilot

_____ **6.** A _____ flies a plane.

_____ **7.** Ten is an _____ number.

_____ **8.** The _____ cries a lot.

_____ **9.** The _____ is black and white.

_____ **10.** A _____ has eight legs.

Home Activity This page practices words with short and long vowels in the first syllable. Work through the items with your child. Ask your child to use three of the words with a short vowel in the first syllable in sentences.

© Pearson Education C

Name_____

Long a Spelled *ai, ay*

Directions Circle the word in ( ) with the **long a** sound. Then write the word on the line.

_____ **1.** Winston always likes to (play/plan) soccer.

_____ **2.** Remember to (slam/say) "thank you."

_____ **3.** Will you (wait/dance) for me after school?

_____ **4.** A (cat/snail) lives in a shell.

_____ **5.** I take a (train/car) to visit my uncle.

_____ **6.** Mom made the pot with (clay/yarn).

Directions Circle the word with the **long a** sound. Then underline the letters that stand for that sound.

7. delay	answer	among
8. cabin	father	okay
9. along	detail	animal
10. raisin	watch	alone
11. finally	subway	half
12. family	because	contain

Home Activity This page practices words with long *a* spelled *ai* and *ay*. Work through the items with your child. Ask your child to collect some magazine pictures of things that have the long *a* sound in their names.

© Pearson Education C

Name_____

Draw Conclusions

- A **conclusion** is a decision you arrive at after you think about what you read.
- You use **details** to help **draw a conclusion.**
- Think about **what you already know** to help you **draw a conclusion.**

Directions Read the story.

Jon was going to the park to skate. He was going with his friend Sara. Before he went out, Jon put on his jacket. Then he put on his scarf and grabbed his gloves. Jon was almost out of the house when he heard his mother say his name. She was holding his hat!

Directions Complete the graphic organizer. Draw a conclusion by circling a sentence in the top box. In the bottom boxes, write details from the story that help you draw the best conclusion.

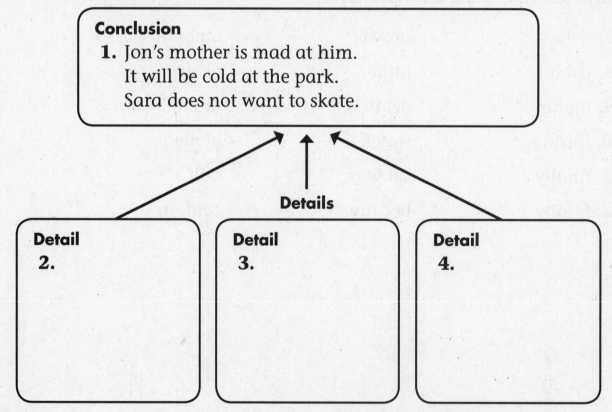

Conclusion
1. Jon's mother is mad at him.
   It will be cold at the park.
   Sara does not want to skate.

Details

Detail 2.

Detail 3.

Detail 4.

Home Activity This page helps your child draw conclusions. Work through the items with your child. Ask your child to read the story on the page again and draw a conclusion about what season it is—summer, fall, winter, or spring. Ask your child how he or she arrived at that conclusion.

Name_____

Vocabulary

Directions Choose the word from the box and write it next to its meaning.

Check the Words You Know

__climate
__extreme
__protection
__shelter
__weather

_____ 1. much more than usual; very great

_____ 2. the sun, wind, or rain in a certain place

_____ 3. the kind of weather a place has

_____ 4. something that covers or protects

_____ 5. act of keeping someone safe from harm

Directions Each sentence has a word missing. Circle the word at the end of each sentence that fits the meaning. Write it on the line.

6. The _____ today is cold and rainy. weather protection

7. A barn is a _____ for animals. climate shelter

8. An umbrella gives _____ from rain. extreme protection

9. Florida has a warm and sunny _____ . climate shelter

10. A thunder storm is _____ weather. protection extreme

Write About Climate

On another paper, write about the climate where you live. Is it often cold, hot, wet, dry, or just right? Write three sentences to describe the climate of the place where you live. Use vocabulary words.

Home Activity This page helps your child read and write vocabulary words. Work through the items with your child. Ask your child if he or she likes the climate where you live and to tell why or why not.

Name_____

Writing

Directions Choose a place with an extreme climate to visit. You can use an idea from the box or another one you like better. Write your ideas on the lines.

> **desert
> Arctic
> deep sea
> shore**

1. I would like to visit _____ .

2. What is extreme about this place?

_____

_____

3. Would you see plants in this place? If so, what kind?

_____

_____

4. What animals would you see in this place? List them.

_____   _____

_____   _____

5. How have animals adapted to this extreme place?

_____

_____

On another paper, describe the plant or animal that you think is most interesting in the extreme place you chose. Tell why it is interesting to you.

© Pearson Education C

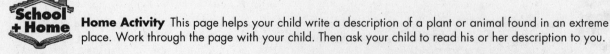

School + Home **Home Activity** This page helps your child write a description of a plant or animal found in an extreme place. Work through the page with your child. Then ask your child to read his or her description to you.

Name_____

Long *e: e, ee, ea*

Directions Circle the word in each sentence that has the same sound as the *e* in *he*. Write the word on the line.

_____ **1.** She wants to plant roses in her garden.

_____ **2.** Will you be coming to my school?

_____ **3.** We are going to the park later today.

_____ **4.** Tim is going to call me after school.

Directions Circle the word in each sentence that has the same sound as the *ee* in *heel*. Write the word on the line.

_____ **5.** Sam will meet Ann at her house to do homework.

_____ **6.** The back wheel on my bike is flat!

_____ **7.** My sister forgot to feed the dog.

_____ **8.** The green apples are the best.

Directions Circle the word in each sentence that has the same sound as the *ea* in *leaf*. Write the word on the line.

_____ **9.** Each student will take the test.

_____ **10.** There are four seats in the room.

_____ **11.** Kara reached for the book on my desk.

_____ **12.** I have to clean my room before dinner.

School + Home Home Activity This page practices words with the long *e* sound as in *me, bee,* and *tea*. Work through the page with your child. Help your child make a list of more words with the long *e* sound.

© Pearson Education C

Name_____

Contractions

Directions Use each pair of words to make a contraction. Write the contraction on the line.

_____ **1.** I will   _____ **6.** do not

_____ **2.** he is   _____ **7.** you will

_____ **3.** let us   _____ **8.** what is

_____ **4.** we will   _____ **9.** are not

_____ **5.** is not   _____ **10.** has not

Directions Use the words in ( ) to make a contraction to complete each sentence. Write the contraction on the line.

_____ **11.** (Here is) the peach tree I planted last fall.

_____ **12.** (It is) full of peaches that are almost ripe.

_____ **13.** (I am) going to pick them for my mother.

_____ **14.** (She is) planning to make a peach pie.

_____ **15.** I (can not) wait!

 Home Activity This page asks your child to form contractions. Ask your child to identify the contractions on this page that are formed with a word plus *not*. Then ask your child to think of other contractions that are formed with a word plus *not*, such as *doesn't*, *shouldn't*, and *couldn't*.

52 Phonics Contractions   **Practice Book Unit 3**

© Pearson Education C

Name_____

Sequence

- **Sequence** is the order of the steps in a process.
- **Clue words**, such as *first, then, before, after,* and *finally,* can tell you when something should be done.

Directions Read the following passage. Then answer the questions below.

Growing plants from seeds is easy. First, find a warm, sunny spot inside. Then fill a very little pot with some dirt. Before you plant, read the seed packet to find out how deep to plant the seeds. Make a little hole in the dirt. Then put two or three seeds in the hole. After you've covered the seeds with dirt, put a little water in the pot. Check the pot each day to see if it needs more water. Finally, plant the plants outside in the garden when they are two or three inches tall.

1. What is the first step to grow a plant from seeds?

_____

2. What is the second step?

_____

3. What do you need to know before you plant the seeds?

_____

4. When should you first water the plant?

_____

5. When should the plant be moved to the garden?

_____

Home Activity This page practices the sequence of steps in a process. Work through the page with your child. Find a recipe for a vegetable dish and help your child prepare it for a family dinner. Use clue words, such as *first, next,* and *then,* as you discuss the recipe with your child.

© Pearson Education C

Name _____

Vocabulary

Directions Match each word from the box with its meaning.
Write the word on the line.

_____ **1.** to become bigger

_____ **2.** the leaves, stems, or other
parts of a plant that
people eat

_____ **3.** what you put a plant in

_____ **4.** the part of a plant that has color

_____ **5.** to put about in different places

Directions Write the word from the box that best matches each
clue below.

6. The plant had a yellow _____ .

7. We will _____ the seeds in the yard.

8. The stem of this plant is a _____ .

9. The plant grows in black _____ .

10. Water and sun help the plant _____ .

Write a Story

Write a short story about a rabbit that grows vegetables in her garden.
Be sure to use as many vocabulary words as possible in your story.

Home Activity This page helps your child learn to read and write the words *flower, grow, scatter, soil,* and
vegetable. Work through the page with your child. Then ask your child to write sentences using each of the
vocabulary words. Encourage him or her to write complete sentences.

Name_____

Writing

Directions First, think about a garden you would like to make. Would it be a vegetable, flower, or rock garden? Would it be on land or a floating garden? Write your choice in the center of the web. Then think about what is special about that garden. Write your ideas in the other circles.

Finally, on another sheet of paper, write three or four sentences about the garden you would like to make. Be sure to tell why it is special. Be sure to start each sentence with a capital letter and to end each sentence with a period.

Home Activity This page helps your child choose a topic to write about and organize the information about that topic. Work through the page with your child. After your child has written the sentences, ask him or her to read the paragraph aloud, listening for ways to improve it.

© Pearson Education C

Name_____

Long o: oa, ow

Directions Circle each word with the **long o** vowel sound as in *goal* and *snow*. Then write the word on the line.

_____ **1.** I will make toast.

_____ **2.** The corn is yellow.

_____ **3.** I can float in the water.

_____ **4.** We like to play in the snow!

_____ **5.** Wash the dog in soap and water.

_____ **6.** I will show you a picture of my cat.

_____ **7.** I saw a rainbow after the storm.

_____ **8.** There are apples in that bowl.

_____ **9.** You can grow plants in the garden.

_____ **10.** Do you know how to ride a horse?

Directions Circle the word in each line with the **long o** vowel sound.

11. goal   among   torn

12. color   gone   grown

13. corn   won   boast

14. worst   coating   corner

15. follow   enjoy   money

Home Activity This page practices words with the long o vowel sound spelled *oa* and *ow*. Work through the items with your child. Ask your child to name the letters in the words in items 11–15 that stand for the long o sound.

© Pearson Education C

Name_____

Contractions 've, 're, 'd

Directions Use each pair of words to make a contraction. Write the contraction on the line. Remember to write an apostrophe (') to stand for missing letters.

1. I have _____

2. you are _____

3. they have _____

4. you have _____

5. they are _____

6. I would _____

7. we have _____

8. you would _____

9. they would _____

10. they have _____

Directions Use the words in ( ) to make a contraction that completes each sentence. Write the contraction on the line.

_____ **11.** (You are) my best friend.

_____ **12.** I asked my mom if (she would) bake cookies.

_____ **13.** (We would) like to play in the park.

_____ **14.** On Saturday (we are) going to the zoo.

_____ **15.** My brother said (he would) fix my bike.

Home Activity This page practices contractions. Work through the items with your child. Ask your child to use the word *I'd* in a sentence to tell what he or she would like to do this weekend.

Main Idea and Supporting Details

- The **main idea** is the most important idea about the topic.
- **Details** are small pieces of information about the main idea.

Directions Read the page from Tina's journal. Then complete the graphic organizer below.

April 12, 2006

Today our class went on a trip to the park by the school. We saw a bird's nest with eggs in it. Our teacher told us it was a robin's nest. We saw animals too—rabbits and ducks. We looked at lots of flowers too.

We hiked to the top of a hill. We sat on the grass in the sun to eat lunch. Some bugs got on me, but that was okay.

I was tired when I got home, but this was the best school trip ever!

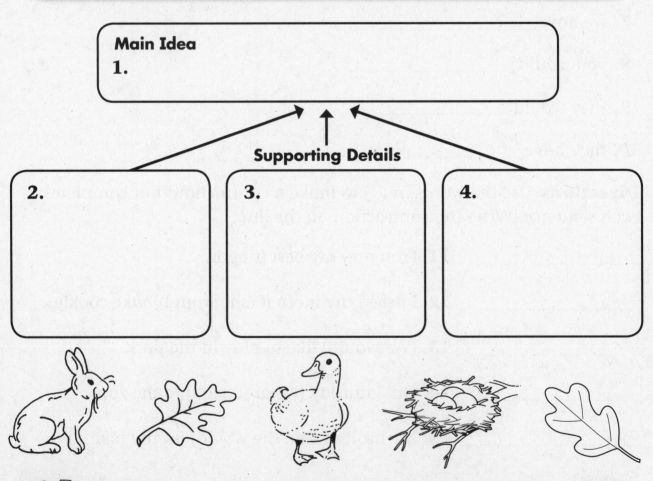

Main Idea

1.

Supporting Details

2.

3.

4.

© Pearson Education C

School + Home **Home Activity** This page helps your child to identify the main idea and details in a passage. Work through the items with your child. Ask your child to read the journal entry again and find other details he or she didn't put in the chart.

Name_____

Vocabulary

Directions Fill in the blank with the word from the box that fits the meaning of the sentence.

Check the Words You Know

__discover
__explain
__myth
__nature
__scientist

1. People made up a _____ to tell why there is thunder.

2. If you don't understand the question, the teacher will _____ it.

3. Plants and animals are part of _____ .

4. One kind of _____ studies the sky.

5. Maybe he will _____ a new planet!

Directions Draw a line from the word to its definition.

6. nature   to see or learn of for the first time

7. discover   a story that tries to explain something in nature

8. scientist   the living things in the outside world

9. explain   to make plain or easy to understand

10. myth   a person who knows lots of science

Write an Interview

On another paper, write four questions you would like to ask a scientist who studies nature. Use as many vocabulary words as possible.

© Pearson Education C

School + Home

Home Activity This page helps your child read and write vocabulary words. Work through the items with your child. Then ask your child to read his or her interview to you.

Name_____

Writing

Directions Think about nature and what would be fun to study. Look at the words in the box for ideas. Then answer the questions.

an animal	weather
a plant	a germ
the sky	the earth
the water	rocks

1. What would you want to study?

_____

2. Is your idea too big? You can't study animals because there are thousands of them. You would have to choose one. Write a smaller topic if yours was too big.

_____

3. What questions about your topic would you like to answer?

_____

_____

_____

4. Why do you think being a scientist would be fun?

_____

_____

_____

On another paper, write about being a scientist. Use your answers to the questions above to help you tell what you would like to explain and what you would hope to discover. Tell why you would enjoy it. Be sure all your words are spelled correctly.

Home Activity This page helps your child write about being a scientist. Work through the page with your child. Then ask your child to read his or her description to you.

© Pearson Education C

Name _____

Draw Conclusions

- A **conclusion** is a decision you reach after you think about details and facts.
- As you read, think about the details and facts and **what you already know** to draw conclusions about what you read.

Directions Read the following passage. Then complete the diagram below to draw a conclusion about Jean.

Jean worked very hard to train for the big race. She did not want to settle for last place. So she got up early every morning to run before school. Each day she ran a little faster. She also ran after school.

Each day she could run a little bit longer. She made sure to eat well and get enough sleep. On the day of the race, Jean knew she was going to win.

Facts and Details
1.

Facts and Details
2.

Facts and Details
3.

Conclusion
4.

© Pearson Education C

School + Home **Home Activity** This page practices drawing conclusions. Work through the page with your child. Ask your child to add to the story about Jean by coming up with other details that would support the conclusion he or she drew about the story.

Name_____

Vocabulary

Directions Match each word with its meaning. Write the word on the line.

_____ **1.** in danger of no longer living or existing

_____ **2.** a huge gray animal with a long trunk and tusks

_____ **3.** to go out of sight; to be gone

_____ **4.** no longer living or existing

_____ **5.** to save from harm

Check the Words You Know

__elephant
__endangered
__extinct
__rescue
__vanish

Directions Write the word from the box that best completes each sentence.

6. Some animals are _____ because of polluted water and air.

7. Others, like the _____ , are hunted for their parts.

8. People and groups are coming to their _____ .

9. They don't want these animals to _____ from the Earth.

10. They are protecting these animals so that they do not become _____ .

Home Activity This page helps your child read and write vocabulary words. Work through the items with your child. Then ask your child to write sentences using each of the vocabulary words. Remind him or her to write complete sentences.

© Pearson Education C

Writing

Directions Read the problems below. Then think about a solution to each problem. Write your solutions in the solution boxes.

Problem
People and factories dump garbage into rivers and lakes. The garbage endangers animals.

↓

Solution

_____

_____

Problem
Elephants are killed for their tusks. People make things from the tusks and sell them for a lot of money.

↓

Solution

_____

_____

On another sheet of paper, write about what people in your community can do to help protect endangered animals. Use your ideas in the diagram. Be sure to start each sentence with a capital letter and end each sentence with a period.

© Pearson Education C

School + Home
Home Activity This page helps your child think of solutions to problems that are facing endangered animals. Work through the page with your child. Discuss your child's solutions to the problems.

Name_____

Diphthongs *ou, ow* /ou/

Directions Circle the word with **ou** or **ow** that has the same vowel sound as **out.** Write the word on the line.

_____ **1.** Jan said, "Ouch!" when she fell on the ice.

_____ **2.** I found two pennies in my pocket.

_____ **3.** My kitten has brown fur.

_____ **4.** There are gray clouds in the sky.

_____ **5.** I don't want to go to sleep now!

_____ **6.** Some animals growl when they are angry.

_____ **7.** A rose is my favorite flower.

_____ **8.** Your house is across the street.

_____ **9.** There is ice on the ground.

_____ **10.** Mary lives around the corner.

Directions Circle each word with the same vowel sound as the first word. Underline the letters that stand for the vowel sound.

11. around	enough	mound	touch
12. town	amount	you	bought
13. bounce	could	grow	howling
14. allow	thought	our	young
15. powder	surround	group	country

© Pearson Education C

Home Activity This page practices words with *ou* and *ow* with the vowel sound in *out*. Work through the items with your child. Ask your child to write this sentence: *I found a brown crayon on the ground.* Ask him or her to underline the letters that make the vowel sound in *out*.

Name_____

Suffixes *-ly, -ful*

Directions Add the suffix **-ly** or **-ful** to each base word. Write the new word on the line.

1. cheer + ful = _____

2. nice + ly = _____

3. happy + ly = _____

4. power + ful = _____

5. sad + ly = _____

6. thank + ful = _____

7. sudden + ly = _____

8. lucky + ly = _____

Directions Add **-ly** or **-ful** to the base word in ( ) to best complete each sentence. Write the new word on the line.

_____ 9. Be (care) when you use scissors.

_____ 10. I ran (quick) in the race.

_____ 11. The flowers in the garden are (color).

_____ 12. A snail moves (slow).

Home Activity This page practices words with the suffix *-ly* or *-ful*. Work through the items with your child. Say the words *wonder, wild, warm,* and *usual.* Ask your child to write new words with the suffix *-ly* or *-ful.*

© Pearson Education C

Name_____

Compare and Contrast

- When you **compare and contrast,** you tell how things are alike and different.
- You can use a **Venn diagram** to **compare and contrast.**

Directions Read the passage.

We used to live on the East Coast. There were many bad storms! The storms had strong winds and heavy rain. Sometimes we covered our windows so they wouldn't break. We worried a little about our house. We stayed inside until the bad weather was over. Sometimes, we got into our car and drove to a safer place.

Now we live on the West Coast. We have earthquakes here. The ground shakes. The windows rattle in our home. Sometimes cups and plates fall off the table! We worry a little about a big earthquake. We believe that our house will not fall down. We run outside to keep safe. But usually the earthquake is a small one.

Directions Use the words in the box to complete the Venn diagram.

go outside	cover windows
ground shakes	worry a little
heavy rain	try to be safe
windows rattle	strong winds
stay inside	things fall off tables

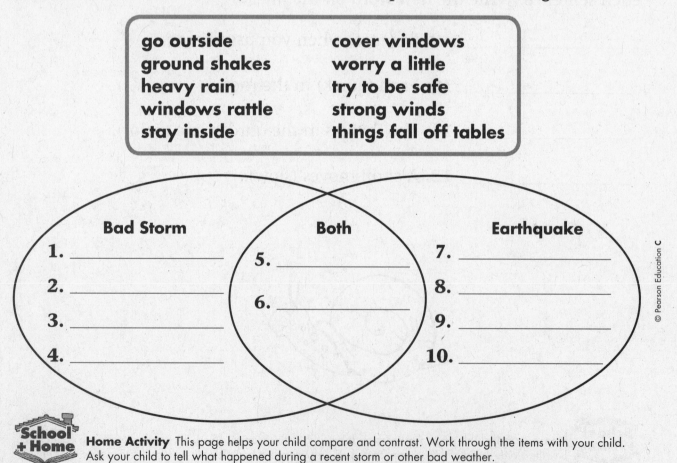

Bad Storm
1. _____
2. _____
3. _____
4. _____

Both
5. _____
6. _____

Earthquake
7. _____
8. _____
9. _____
10. _____

© Pearson Education C

School + Home **Home Activity** This page helps your child compare and contrast. Work through the items with your child. Ask your child to tell what happened during a recent storm or other bad weather.

Name_____

Vocabulary

Directions Write the word from the box that fits each sentence.

1. You can see many plants and animals
   _____ .

2. I know what tree frogs look like, so I can
   _____ them.

3. Some parks have lots of _____
   flowers in the spring.

4. Deer _____ the forest behind
   my home.

5. A pond is a frog's _____ environment.

Directions Draw a line from the word to its meaning.

6. recognize   very pleasing to see or hear

7. outdoors   to live in

8. inhabit   not made by people

9. beautiful   outside

10. natural   to know you have seen something before

Write a Travel Ad

On a separate sheet of paper, write an ad for a place in nature. Your ad should try to get people to visit this place. Use as many vocabulary words as you can.

© Pearson Education C

Home Activity This page helps your child read and write vocabulary words. Work through the items with your child. Then have your child read his or her travel ad to you.

Name_____

Writing

Directions Choose a place in nature that you would like to visit. You can use an idea from the box or another one you like better. Write the place in nature in the center oval. In each of the other ovals, write how it looks, the sounds you would hear, the kinds of plants it has, and the kinds of animals you might see.

wetland	rain forest
forest	nature center

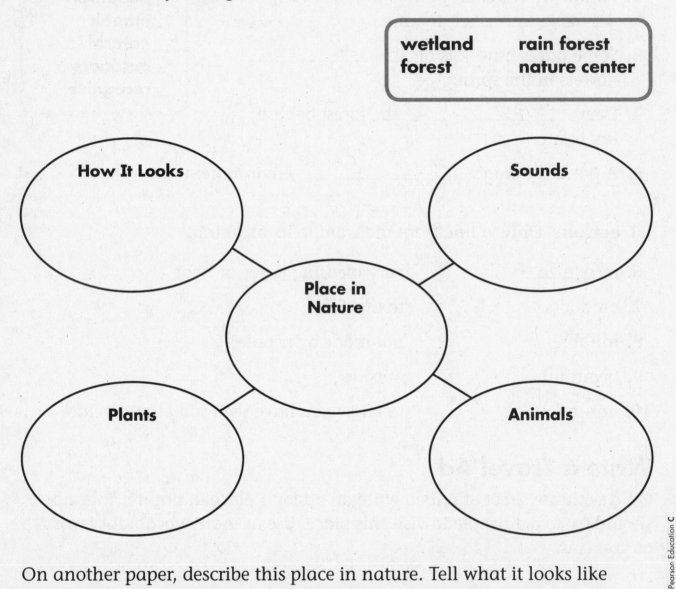

How It Looks

Sounds

Place in Nature

Plants

Animals

On another paper, describe this place in nature. Tell what it looks like and sounds like. Tell why it is fun to visit. Use some vocabulary words. Check the spelling of all your words.

© Pearson Education C

School + Home **Home Activity** This page helps your child write a description of a place in nature. Work through the page with your child. Then ask your child to read his or her description to you.

Name_____

Diphthongs *oi, oy*

Directions Circle each word with **oi** or **oy** that has the same vowel sound as **toy**. Then write the word on the line.

_____ **1.** Kenny found a jar of coins.

_____ **2.** He had saved them when he was a little boy.

_____ **3.** He felt joyful.

_____ **4.** Maybe now he could get the robot toy.

_____ **5.** The "Your Choice" store sells robots.

_____ **6.** One robot had a loud voice.

_____ **7.** It made a beeping noise.

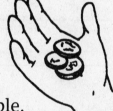

_____ **8.** Kenny joined his sister at the table.

_____ **9.** He told her he would enjoy the robot.

_____ **10.** She pointed to the jar.

_____ **11.** To spend the coins would be bad.

_____ **12.** It could spoil the set that they had.

Home Activity This page practices words with the *oy* sound heard in *toy* and *boil*. Work through the items with your child. Help your child write and talk about words with the vowel sound in *toy* or *boil*, such as *boy*, *joy*, *enjoy*, *annoy*, *foil*, *moist*, *toil*, and *loyal*.

Name_____

Prefixes *un-*, *re-*

Directions Add the prefix **un-** or **re-** to each base word. Write the new word on the line.

1. un- + lock = _____

2. re- + fill = _____

3. un- + like = _____

4. re- + draw = _____

Directions Write the word from the box that best fits each definition.

_____ 5. to do again

_____ 6. not safe

_____ 7. to write again

_____ 8. not common

uncommon
rewrite
redo
unsafe

Directions Add the prefix **un-** or **re-** to the word in ( ) to complete each sentence. Write the new word on the line.

_____ 9. It is time to (load) the truck.

_____ 10. I will (draw) part of my picture.

Home Activity This page practices words with the prefixes *un- (unlock)* and *re- (replay)*. Work through the items with your child. Help your child to choose words from the box above and use them in sentences.

Name_____

Sequence

- **Sequence** is the order in a story—what happens first, next, and last.
- Sometimes **clue words** can tell you what happens *first, next,* and *last.*

Directions Read this passage. Then answer the questions below.

Lin had a plan to win the race. She would not run her fastest at the beginning. If she ran the whole race at top speed, she would be tired. Let the other girls get tired! Then Lin could run very fast and win. The sound of a horn started the race. At first, speedy Carla ran quickly and led the runners. Then Carla slowed down about halfway around the track. That is when Lin pushed herself to run faster. She passed two other runners. Next she passed Carla. Carla tried to catch up. Near the finish line, Carla was getting close. Lin felt her legs move even faster. Finally she crossed the line and won.

1. Did Lin have her plan before the race or when the race had started?

_____

2. Who was the first runner to lead the race?

_____

3. What did Lin do when the leader slowed down?

_____

4. What did Carla do when Lin began running faster?

_____

5. What clue word tells you that Lin's winning was the last part of the race?

_____

School + Home **Home Activity** This page allows your child to identify a sequence of events in a story. Work through the items with your child. Then ask your child to help you make up another story about a race and tell what happens first, next, and last.

Name_____

Vocabulary

Check the Words You Know

_audience   _perform
_famous   _talent
_instrument _unique

Directions Fill in the blank with the word that fits the meaning of the sentence. Write the word on the line.

1. What is your special _____?

2. Do you play music in your own _____ way?

3. What _____ do you know how to play?

4. Do you ever _____ in a show?

5. Who is in your _____, besides your family?

6. Maybe some day you will become a _____ movie star.

Directions Draw a line from each word to its meaning.

7. instrument   having lots of fans

8. audience   one of a kind

9. famous   something used to make sounds

10. unique   people gathered to hear or see something

Write an Advertisement

On a separate sheet of paper, write an ad for someone with a unique talent who performs for others. Use as many of the vocabulary words as you can.

© Pearson Education C

Name_____

Writing

Directions Describe a musical instrument.
You can tell what the instrument looks like
and how it sounds.

What kind of instrument will you describe?

strings	brass	drum
bow	tune	strum
beat	voice	hum
twang	chime	honk
noise	piping	joyful

_____

1. Circle any words from the box that can help describe the instrument.

2. Write other words that you can use to describe the instrument or
   how it sounds.

_____

_____

Now write ideas to use in your description.

3. What does the instrument look like?

_____

4. How does the instrument sound?

_____

5. Why do you like this instrument?

_____

6. Write a good sentence that you might use to begin your description.

_____

On another paper, write your description. Identify the instrument and
describe it. Tell why you like it. Make sure you use capital letters and
punctuation correctly.

© Pearson Education C

Home Activity This page helps your child write a description. Work through the page with your child. Then
have your child read the description aloud.

Name _____

Vowels *oo* in *moon*

Directions Circle the words in the box that have the same sound as the **oo** in **moon**. Then write the words on the lines.

four	too
noon	soon
shoot	took
boat	look
good	zoo

1. _____

2. _____

3. _____

4. _____

5. _____

Directions Write the new words on the line.

6. Change the *c* in *cool* to *sch*.

   What is the new word? _____

7. Change the *b* in *boot* to *r*.

   What is the new word? _____

8. Change the *l* in *loose* to *m*.

   What is the new word? _____

9. Change the *d* in *food* to *l*.

   What is the new word? _____

10. Change the *t* in *tool* to *st*.

    What is the new word? _____

Home Activity This page practices words with the sound of *oo* as in *moon*. Play a rhyming game with your child. Ask him or her to give rhyming words for *moon*, *room*, and *pool*.

© Pearson Education C

Name _____

Silent Consonants *kn, gn, mb*

Directions Read the story. Underline the words with the silent consonants **mb**, **kn**, and **gn**. Then write the underlined words on the lines.

> The sign on the knob said, "Class Meets Here." Maria wanted to learn to knit. She knew it would be fun. She knocked and she went in. Maria learned how to tie a knot in the yarn. Then she learned how to use her thumb to move the yarn. The yarn is as soft as a lamb. Maria was going to make a pair of knee socks. She worked hard until her fingers were numb.

1. _____   6. _____

2. _____   7. _____

3. _____   8. _____

4. _____   9. _____

5. _____   10. _____

Directions Read each word. Underline the silent consonants. Then write the word.

11. gnat   _____

12. crumb   _____

13. know   _____

14. thumb   _____

15. gnome   _____

Home Activity This page practices words with silent consonants. Work through the items with your child. Use a dictionary and help your child name additional words that start with *kn* and *gn*.

© Pearson Education C

Name _____

Compare and Contrast

- When you **compare and contrast,** you tell how things are alike and how they are different.
- You can use a **Venn diagram** to **compare and contrast.**
- Reading slowly helps you **notice details, key words, or other clues** the author uses in **comparing** and **contrasting.**

Directions Read the following passage. Then complete the diagram to compare and contrast what you read. Use these words: *paint, dance, slide, swings, school, race.*

Linda and Nan live on the same street. They like to go to school together. They often do different things. Linda likes to paint pictures. Nan likes to dance. When school is over, Linda and Nan play at the park. Nan likes to play on the slide. Linda likes to play on the swings. Both of the girls like to race around the path in the park.

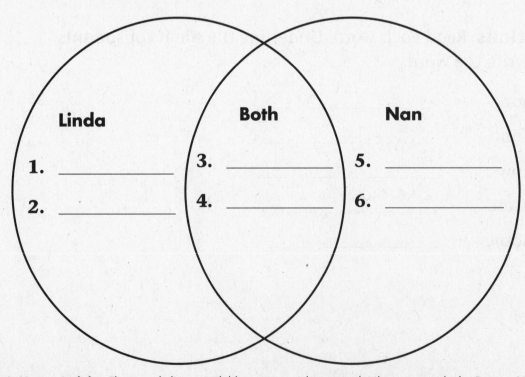

Linda

1. _____
2. _____

Both

3. _____
4. _____

Nan

5. _____
6. _____

© Pearson Education C

Home Activity The page helps your child compare and contrast the things two girls do. Draw a Venn diagram together. Write "Playing Outside" in the first circle, "Playing Inside" in the second circle, and "Both" where the two circles overlap. Ask your child to use the diagram to list games they play outside and inside and in both places.

Name _____

Vocabulary

Directions Solve each riddle with a word from the box. Write the word on the line.

Check the Words You Know

_depth
_height
_peak
_position
_scale
_summit

1. I tell how high something is.

   What am I? _____

2. I tell how deep something is.

   What am I? _____

3. I am the top of a very high hill.

   What am I? _____

4. I am another word for climb.

   What am I? _____

5. I am the highest point at the top of the very high hill.

   What am I? _____

Directions Write the word from the box that best completes each sentence below.

6. Marcus is going to _____ Mount Logan.

7. It is over 5,000 feet in _____.

8. He cannot see its _____.

9. It will be a long climb to the _____.

10. Marcus gets himself into _____ and begins to climb.

School + Home   **Home Activity** The page helps your child read and write vocabulary words. Ask your child to use this week's vocabulary words in sentences.

Name _____

Writing

Directions Think of questions for an interview. Write ideas on the lines.

1. Do you plan to interview a mountain climber or a free diver? Write your answer on the line.

_____

2. Circle the words that describe what you want to know.

age   practice   clothes   name   school

training   tools   place   lessons   feelings

3. Make a list of other things you'd like to know.

_____

_____

_____

4. Most questions begin with the words *who, what, when, where,* and *how.* Circle the three words you will use in your questions.

who   what   when   where   how

5. Write three questions to use in the interview. Be sure to use a question mark at the end of each question.

_____

_____

_____

_____

Home Activity This page helps your child write questions for an interview. Work through the page with your child. Then have your child write three questions to ask you about your work or your favorite type of recreation.

© Pearson Education C

Name _____

Vowel Patterns *ew, ue*

Directions Circle the word with **ew** or **ue** in each sentence. Then write the word on the line.

_____ **1.** Roy got a new jacket for school.

_____ **2.** Jane used a blue crayon to draw a river.

_____ **3.** Are 100 pennies many or a few?

_____ **4.** The stew has meat in it.

_____ **5.** Bob threw the toy to his dog.

_____ **6.** I used glue to put pictures on the page.

Directions Circle the word with **ew** or **ue**.

7. clue	laugh	people
8. draw	crew	heavy
9. true	money	you're
10. though	eight	blue
11. world	dew	found
12. woman	usual	knew

© Pearson Education C

Home Activity This page practices words with the vowel patterns *ew* and *ue*. Work through the items with your child. Ask your child to name as many things as possible that are blue.

Name _____

Silent Consonants *st*, *wr*

Directions Choose the word in ( ) with the silent consonant, as in **st** or **wr**, to complete each sentence. Write the word on the line.

_____ **1.** Be careful! Don't (wreck, crack) the window.

_____ **2.** I want to (tell, write) a story about a dog that can fly.

_____ **3.** Pat is (listening, dancing) to the music.

_____ **4.** The snow is (melting, glistening) in the sun.

_____ **5.** You wear a watch on your (leg, wrist).

_____ **6.** The king and queen lived in a (castle, house).

Directions Circle each word in the box that has a silent consonant, as in **st** or **wr**. Write the circled words on the lines below.

bottle	thistle
bustle	coins
thousand	whistle
famous	wrap
wrench	pursue
shrewd	wring

st

7. _____

8. _____

9. _____

wr

10. _____

11. _____

12. _____

School + Home **Home Activity** This page practices words with the silent consonants *st* and *wr*. Work through the items with your child. Ask your child to write a sentence using the word *whistle*, and then read the sentence aloud.

© Pearson Education C

Name _____

Draw Conclusions

- A **conclusion** is a decision you reach after thinking about what you read.
- You use **what you already know** to help you draw a conclusion.
- You **ask yourself,** "Does my conclusion make sense?"

Directions Read the following passage. Then answer the questions below.

> My friends and I started a nature-writing club. We asked our parents to join us.
>
> We hiked in a different state park every week. We saw lakes, rivers, and streams. We saw leafy trees, green grasses, and flowers. We saw insects, birds, frogs, turtles, and small mammals. Sometimes, Mike went fishing, but no one else did.
>
> While we were there, we wrote about what we saw. After we had been to ten parks, we put our writing together to make a book.

1. Why do you think these friends wanted to start a nature-writing club?

_____

2. Why did they invite their parents to join them?

_____

3. What do you think they wrote about?

_____

4. Who most likely wrote about what it's like to go fishing? Explain.

_____

5. Write a question about the book the club members made. Then draw a conclusion to answer your question.

_____

_____

 Home Activity This page allows your child to draw conclusions. Work through the items with your child. Ask your child if he or she thinks the writing club members hiked in the winter or summer and explain why.

© Pearson Education C

Name _____

Vocabulary

Directions Write the vocabulary word from the box next to its meaning.

_____ **1.** great joy

_____ **2.** hardly ever seen, found, or happening

_____ **3.** a group of things that go together

_____ **4.** a feeling of wanting to know or share in

_____ **5.** not common

_____ **6.** more than usual; different from others

Check the Words You Know

__collection
__delight
__interest
__rare
__special
__unusual

Directions Write the word from the box that fits in each sentence.

7. Bea has a _____ of many different plants.

8. She has an _____ in things from nature.

9. It is a joy, or _____ , to find a new plant.

10. Some of her plants are common, but others are _____ .

Write a Description

On a separate paper, write about something fun to collect. Tell why. Use as many of the vocabulary words as you can.

© Pearson Education C

School + Home **Home Activity** This page helps your child read and write vocabulary words. Work through the items with your child. Ask your child to circle the vocabulary words in his or her description and tell what they mean.

Name _____

Writing

Think about a hobby you have or a hobby that you would enjoy. Think of words to make the hobby sound like fun.

Directions Circle any words from the box that you can use to describe your hobby.

Now answer these questions.

delight	unusual
interest	unique
exciting	collection

1. What is the hobby?

_____

2. How did you learn to do it?

_____

_____

3. What do you like best about the hobby?

_____

_____

4. Would your friends enjoy this hobby too? Explain.

_____

_____

5. Write a good sentence to begin your description.

_____

_____

On another paper, write about your hobby. Tell why you like it. Make sure your words are spelled correctly.

© Pearson Education C

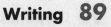

Home Activity This page helps your child write a description. Work through the page with your child. Then have your child read the description aloud.

Name _____

Vowels *oo* in *foot, u* in *put*

Directions Circle each word with the vowel sound in **foot** and **put**. Then write the word on the line.

_____ **1.** Ben stood up when it was his turn to read.

_____ **2.** I took a trip to the beach.

_____ **3.** The glass is full of milk.

_____ **4.** Our desks are made of wood.

_____ **5.** Look for the box under the bed.

_____ **6.** Lin's jacket has a hood to keep her warm.

Directions Circle the words in the box that have the vowel sound in **foot** and **put.** Write the words on the lines below.

7. _____

8. _____

9. _____

10. _____

11. _____

12. _____

book	moon
cookie	pull
foot	school
four	use
good	wool
hundred	sun

Home Activity This page practices words with the vowel sound in *foot* and *put*. Work through the page with your child. Ask your child to say one sentence using the word *pudding* and another sentence using the word *hook*.

Name _____

Suffixes -ness, -less

Directions Add the suffix **-ness** or **-less** to each word. Write the new word on the line.

1. pain + -less = _____

2. bold + -ness = _____

3. end   + -less = _____

4. fair + -ness = _____

5. care + -less = _____

6. happy + -ness = _____

7. worth + -less = _____

8. good + -ness = _____

Directions Add **-less** or **-ness** to the word in ( ) to complete each sentence. Write the new word on the line.

harmless
illness
sadness
useless

_____ 9. You stay home from school when you have an (ill).

_____ 10. Most spiders are (harm). They won't hurt you.

_____ 11. A nail without a point is (use).

_____ 12. Sue felt (sad) when her friend moved away.

© Pearson Education C

 School + Home **Home Activity** This page practices words with the suffixes *-ness* and *-less*. Work through the page with your child. Ask your child to do something that shows silliness and then write a sentence to tell what he or she did.

Name _____

Compare and Contrast

- When you **compare and contrast,** you tell how things are alike and how they are different.
- You can use a **Venn diagram** to **compare and contrast.**

Directions Complete the Venn diagram to compare and contrast. Use the words from the box to compare the two games.

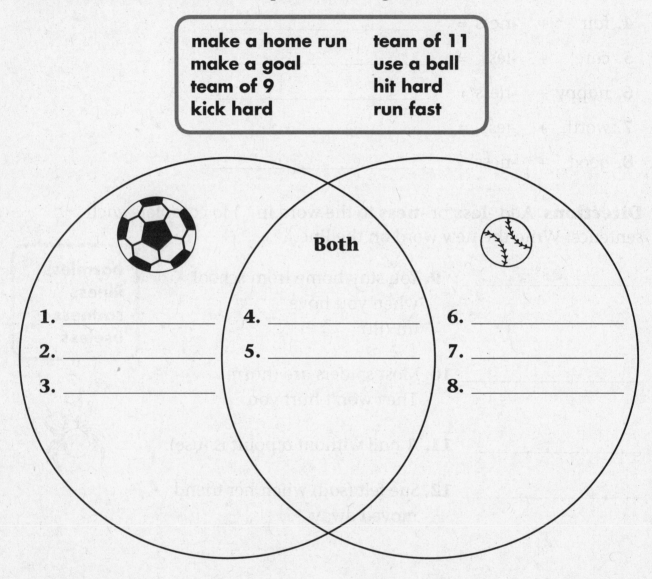

make a home run   team of 11
make a goal   use a ball
team of 9   hit hard
kick hard   run fast

Both

1. _____   4. _____   6. _____
2. _____   5. _____   7. _____
3. _____   8. _____

© Pearson Education C

Home Activity This page helps your child compare and contrast two games. Work through the page with your child. Draw a Venn diagram. Label the parts "Snow," "Both," and "Rain." Help your child complete the diagram.

Name _____

Vocabulary

Directions Write the vocabulary word from the box next to its meaning.

_____ **1.** a place where water falls from a high place

_____ **2.** a try; an effort

_____ **3.** the space in between

_____ **4.** worthy of notice; unusual

_____ **5.** an unusual or thrilling journey

_____ **6.** not able to be or happen

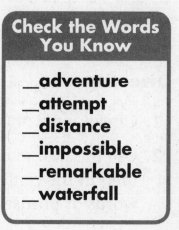

Check the Words You Know

__adventure
__attempt
__distance
__impossible
__remarkable
__waterfall

Directions Write the word from the box that best fits the meaning of the sentence.

7. It is a long _____ from Earth to the moon.

8. Taking a raft down the river would be a thrilling _____ !

9. You can get wet if you stand near a _____ .

10. I made an _____ to stand on my head, but I fell!

Write a Description

On a separate paper, write about an adventure you would like to have. Use as many of the vocabulary words as you can.

Home Activity This page helps your child read and write vocabulary words. Work through the items with your child. Ask your child if the adventure he or she wrote about is possible or impossible and tell why.

© Pearson Education C

Name _____

Writing

A world record is something you do first or something you do best. Think about what would be fun to do.

Directions

1. Circle any words from the box that you might use.

2. Use the web to help you. Write your world record idea in the center oval. In the outside ovals, write words or phrases that tell about the world record.

On another paper, write a paragraph about your world record and how you would set it. Make sure your words are spelled correctly.

biggest
highest
longest
fastest
surprising
adventure
outstanding

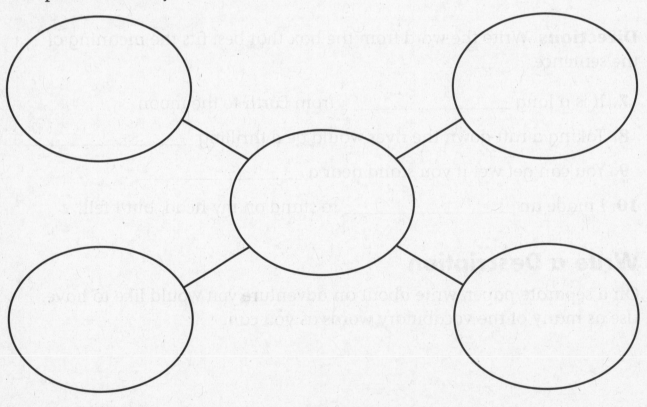

© Pearson Education C

School + Home **Home Activity** This page helps your child write about a world record. Work through the page with your child. Then have your child read the paragraph aloud.

94 Writing

Practice Book Unit 4

Name _____

Short e: ea

Directions Choose the word in each group with the **short e** sound spelled **ea**. Write the word on the line.

_____ 1. clean   spread   each

_____ 2. search   greed   weather

_____ 3. freeze   beach   death

_____ 4. instead   teach   preach

_____ 5. reaching   steady   screeching

_____ 6. deaf   pioneer   creature

> **bread**
> **head**
> **sweater**
> **thread**

Directions Choose a word from the box that names the picture. Be sure the word you choose has the **short e** sound spelled **ea.**

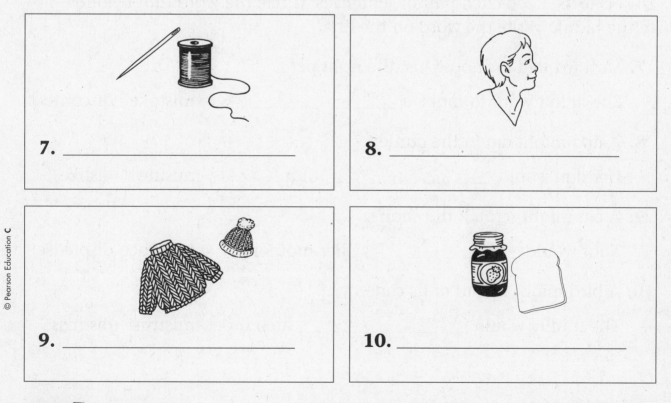

7. _____

8. _____

9. _____

10. _____

Home Activity This page practices words with the short e sound spelled *ea* as in *bread*. Work through the page with your child. Have your child write five sentences using words from this page with the short e sound spelled *ea*.

© Pearson Education C

Name _____

Prefixes *mis-*, *dis-*

- A **prefix** is a syllable added to the beginning of a word. Prefixes can help you figure out the meaning of a word you don't know.
- The **prefix** *dis-* means "the opposite of" or "not."
- The **prefix** *mis-* means "bad or badly" or "wrong or wrongly."

Directions Match the word with its meaning.

1. misbehave   to give wrong directions to

2. dismount   to prove wrong

3. dishonest   to behave badly

4. misdirect   to take a wrong step

5. disprove   to show a lack of honesty

6. misstep   to get off something

Directions Read each pair of sentences. Circle the word that belongs in the blank. Write the word on the line.

7. Sara wanted to choose just the right pet.

   She didn't want to make a _____ .   mistake   discontent

8. A dog might dig in the garden.

   Her dad would _____ that.   misfile   dislike

9. A cat might scratch the chairs.

   That would _____ her mother.   misplace   displease

10. A bird might fly out of its cage.

    The family would _____ such a pet.   mistrust   dismiss

Home Activity Your child forms and writes words with the prefixes *dis-* and *mis-* on this page. Work through the page with your child. Then ask your child to write sentences using the words with the prefixes *dis-* and *mis-* in items 1–6.

© Pearson Education C

Name _____

Main Idea

- The **main idea** is the most important idea in a selection or a paragraph.
- The small pieces of information that tell about the main idea are the **supporting details.**

Directions Read the following passage. Then answer the questions below.

> A cat uses its tail to tell people how it feels. A tail that moves back and forth very quickly means that the cat is angry. A tail that slowly moves back and forth means that the cat is happy. A tail tucked between the cat's legs means that the cat is worried. A tail held low to the ground with its hairs fluffed out means that the cat is afraid. And a tail held straight up and still means, "I'm glad to see you." So, if you want to know how a cat is feeling, watch its tail!

1. What is the main idea of the passage?

_____

2. What is one detail that supports the main idea?

_____

3. What is another detail that supports the main idea?

_____

4. What might be a fact you think has been left out of this passage?

_____

5. How do you think the writer knows about how cats use their tails?

_____

Home Activity The activity on this page focuses on the main idea and supporting details. Find a newspaper or magazine advertisement for a product that is being sold in a store. Help your child decide what the ad is about and what the facts are about the product.

© Pearson Education C

Name _____

Vocabulary

Directions Match each word with its meaning. Write the word on the line.

_____ **1.** a living thing grown to full size

_____ **2.** a good chance

_____ **3.** to copy closely, to imitate

_____ **4.** to change to make fit

_____ **5.** to understand clearly

_____ **6.** to give or listen to information

Directions Write the word from the box that best completes each sentence below.

7. Seahorses are really fishes that

_____ very tiny horses.

8. Mates do a greeting dance to

_____ with each other.

9. Baby seahorses must take care of

themselves and _____

to their surroundings.

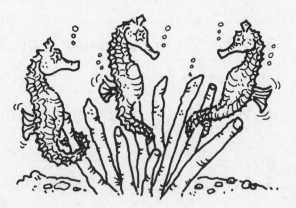

10. Most _____ seahorses

only live to be three years old.

© Pearson Education C

Home Activity This activity helps your child read and write vocabulary words. Ask your child to create a short story. Encourage him or her to use as many vocabulary words as possible.

Name _____

Writing

Directions Think about what you can learn by studying animals.
Answer the following questions.

1. Where can you study animals? Check each place where you might study animals.

   _____ in zoos   _____ in parks

   _____ in backyards   _____ on farms

   _____ in homes   _____ at school

2. What kinds of animals would you see? List two or three animals for each place.

   in zoos _____

   in backyards _____

   in homes _____

   in parks _____

   on farms _____

   at school _____

3. What could you see the animals doing? Check each activity you might see.

   _____ sleeping   _____ playing

   _____ eating   _____ fighting

   _____ running   _____ discovering

   _____ climbing   _____ watching you

On a separate paper, write your answer to the question about what we can learn by studying animals. Make sure you use complete sentences.

© Pearson Education C

School + Home **Home Activity** This page helps your child think of a topic to write about related to studying animals. Watch an animal in your home, outside, or on TV for a few minutes with your child and then discuss what you've observed and what it might mean.

Name_____

Vowel Sound in *ball: a, al*

Directions Choose the word with the vowel sound in *ball*. Write the word on the line.

_____ **1.** We live in a (little, small) house.

_____ **2.** My uncle lives with us (also, too).

_____ **3.** Sometimes we (speak, talk) about getting a bigger home.

_____ **4.** We (almost, around) decided to get a different house.

_____ **5.** We are (always, still) glad that we stayed here.

_____ **6.** This is the place we (sing, call) home.

Directions Write **al** to complete each word. Use the words in the box to help you. Write the whole word on the line.

walk	chalk	fall	halt	tall	wall

_____ **7.** Don't f _ _ l on the ice!

_____ **8.** You can write with ch _ _ k.

_____ **9.** The roof is very t _ _ l.

_____ **10.** The side of a room is a w _ _ l.

_____ **11.** We w _ _ k by the park on our way to school.

_____ **12.** The word h _ _ t means stop.

© Pearson Education C

School + Home **Home Activity** This page practices words that have the vowel sound in *ball*. Work through the page with your child. Ask your child to find a wall, a hall, and something tall in your home.

Name_____

Consonants *ph* /f/, *dge* /j/

Directions Choose the word from the box that matches each word below. Write the missing letters to complete each word. Say each word.

phone	**phony**
photo	**trophy**
graph	

1. t r o _ _ y

2. _ _ o t o

3. g r a _ _

4. _ _ o n y

5. _ _ o n e

trophy

photo

Directions Circle the word that has the *j* sound heard in *jar* or *edge*. Underline the letters that spell the *j* sound.

6. judge	guess	zigzag
7. grade	fudge	north
8. graph	snail	ridge
9. wedge	peach	ouch
10. night	ledge	giggle
11. cowboy	build	bridge
12. badge	wrap	knife

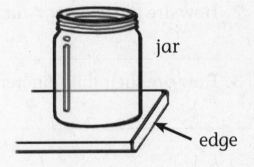
jar

edge

badge

bridge

© Pearson Education C

School + Home

Home Activity This page practices words that have the *f* and *j* sounds spelled *ph* and *dge*. Work through the page with your child. One at a time, say the words *lodge, phase, pledge,* and *phony*. Ask your child to make a fist if he or she hears the *f* sound and to jump if he or she hears the *j* sound.

Name_____

Compare and Contrast

- To **compare and contrast** is to tell how things are alike and different.

Directions Read the following passage. Then answer the questions below.

> Don's dog is white with brown spots. Its fur is soft. It has a long tail. Pete's dog is black. It has soft fur. Its tail is short. Both dogs have loud barks! They both like to play catch, too.

1. How are the colors of Don's dog and Pete's dog different?

_____

_____

2. How are the two dogs' fur alike?

_____

_____

3. How are their tails different?

_____

_____

4. How are their barks the same?

_____

_____

5. Both dogs like to catch a ball. Does this show a way they are alike or different? Tell how you know.

_____

_____

_____

© Pearson Education C

School + Home **Home Activity** This page is about comparing and contrasting. Name your child's two favorite sandwiches. Talk about how they are alike and different.

Name_____

Vocabulary

Directions Draw a line to match each word with its definition.

Check the Words You Know

__clothing
__custom
__decade
__ordinary
__style
__tradition

1. custom   things to put on, like shirts

2. ordinary   ten years of time

3. tradition   a special way that people dress

4. decade   not special; common; everyday

5. clothing   the handing down of customs

6. style   a common way of doing something

Directions Write the word from the box that answers each question.

7. What is ten years?

_____

8. What do you put on?

_____

9. What is a word for something that is not special?

_____

10. What is something that many people do again and again?

_____

© Pearson Education C

Home Activity This page helps your child read and write vocabulary words. Work through the items with your child. Then help your child think of customs in your family.

Writing

Think about the clothing you wear when it is cold. Compare and contrast it with the clothing you wear when it is hot.

Directions Write a paragraph about what people wear when it is hot outside. Also tell what people wear when it is cold outside.

same	jeans	clothing
different	top	mittens
coat	scarf	shorts
shirt	boots	

1. Circle any words from the box that you might use.

2. What can you wear on hot and cold days?

_____

_____

3. What would you wear only on hot days?

_____

_____

4. Write two things you need when it is cold.

_____

_____

5. Write a good sentence to begin your paragraph.

_____

_____

On another paper, write your paragraph. Compare and contrast clothes for hot days and cold days. Make sure your words are spelled correctly.

School + Home **Home Activity** This page helps your child write sentences about a topic. Work through the page with your child. Then have your child read the paragraph aloud.

© Pearson Education C

Name_____

Vowel Sound in *ball:* au, aw

Directions Choose the word in each group with the vowel sound in **ball**. Write the word on the line.

_____ 1. law   farm   act

_____ 2. mad   pause   want

_____ 3. take   place   haul

_____ 4. hawk   parents   class

_____ 5. wrap   yawn   start

_____ 6. auto   day   hard

draw

Directions Write **au** or **aw** to complete each word. Use the word box to help you. Write the whole word on the line to the left.

| awful | because | straw | draw | lawn | saw |

_____ 7. I s_____ a new book I wanted to read.

_____ 8. I wanted to read it bec_____se it was about horses.

_____ 9. The horses eat hay and sleep on str_____ .

_____ 10. I think I will dr_____ a picture of a horse.

_____ 11. The horse can stand on the l_____n by the barn.

_____ 12. I hope my picture does not look _____ful.

© Pearson Education C

Home Activity This page practices words with the vowel sound in *ball* spelled *au* or *aw*. Work through the page with your child. Ask your child to make a list of the words with the vowel sound in *ball* spelled *aw* word then add more words to the list.

Name_____

Suffixes -er, -or

Directions Add the suffix to each base word.
Write the new word on the line.

1. farm + -er = _____

2. act + -or = _____

3. sail + -or = _____

4. teach + -er = _____

5. visit + -or = _____

6. play + -er = _____

Directions Write the word from the box that best fits each definition.

_____ 7. one who ships packages

_____ 8. a person who makes new things

_____ 9. one between the ages of 13 and 19

_____ 10. one who writes books

_____ 11. an artist

_____ 12. a person who directs

| director |
| painter |
| shipper |
| teenager |
| inventor |
| writer |

Home Activity The activity uses words with the suffixes -er and -or. Work through the page with your child. Then work together to write definitions for the words in items 1–6.

© Pearson Education C

Name_____

Draw Conclusions

A **conclusion** is a decision you reach after you think about details or facts in what you read and what you already know.

Directions Read the following passage. Then answer the questions.

If you could live anywhere, what place would you choose?

Would you choose a hot country? There is sunshine every day. You could play at the seashore and swim. You could fish in the lakes. You could plant crops that grow fast in the sunshine.

Would you choose a country where it is cold all the time? You could play in the snow. You could skate on the ice. You could use your sled to ride down the hills. You would have to keep on lots of clothes.

Or, would you choose the United States? You already know a lot about life in the United States because you live here!

1. Would a hot place be a good place for someone who likes to cook and eat outside? Why or why not?

_____

2. Would a hot place be a good place for someone who likes to skate and ice-fish? Why or why not?

_____

3. Would a very cold place be a good home for someone who likes to plant and grow crops? Why or why not?

_____

4. Would a very cold place be a good home for someone who likes to swim outside? Why or why not?

_____

5. Which place would you choose to live? Why?

_____

Home Activity This activity asks questions about a story that requires drawing conclusions. Give your child a faulty conclusion, such as "I want some groceries, so I think I'll go to a movie." Ask your child to correct the sentence and give a reason.

© Pearson Education C

Name_____

Vocabulary

Directions Match each word from the box with its meaning.
Write the word on the line.

Check the Words You Know

__country   __popular
__culture   __similar
__language   __transfer

_____ **1.** the speech used by a group of people

_____ **2.** much the same

_____ **3.** the land of a group of people

_____ **4.** liked by most people

_____ **5.** the customs of a group of people

_____ **6.** to move from one place to another

Directions Write the word from the box that best completes each
question below.

7. What _____ do they speak?

8. What is a _____ sport that everyone likes?

9. What _____ do we live in?

10. Is Japan _____ to or different from the
United States?

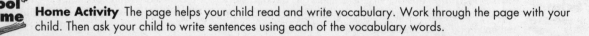

Home Activity The page helps your child read and write vocabulary. Work through the page with your
child. Then ask your child to write sentences using each of the vocabulary words.

© Pearson Education C

Name_____

Writing

Directions You need to decide what to write about. Read the questions below. Write answers to the questions to get ideas for your letter.

1. What is a new sport? _____

2. What is a new kind of music? _____

3. What is a new game? _____

4. What is a new kind of food? _____

5. What is a new clothing style? _____

Directions Fill in the blanks below with the words you will use for each part of your letter.

• The **heading** gives the reader your address. It also tells when you wrote the letter. What heading will you use in your letter?

My street address: _____

Today's date: _____

• The **greeting** opens the letter. It is a way to say "hello" to the person you are writing to. What greeting will you use in your letter?

Dear _____ ,

• The **body** is the main part of the letter. (You'll write this later.)

• The **closing** ends the letter. It says "good-bye." You might close your letter by writing something like "Your pen pal." What closing will you use?

_____

• The **signature** is your name. When writing to friends or family, use your first name. When writing to someone you don't know very well, you should use your full name. How will you sign your letter?

_____

On another sheet of paper, write your letter. Be sure to include all the parts of a letter.

Home Activity This page helps your child write a letter to someone about something new in America. Help your child write a letter to a student in another country asking questions about the country's culture. The questions might be about sports, food, clothing, or music.

Name_____

Vowel Sound in *ball*: *augh, ough*

Directions Circle the word with the vowel sound in **ball** to complete each sentence. Write the word on the line.

_____ **1.** Lu and I (decided/thought) we were different.

_____ **2.** He (threw/caught) baseballs with his left hand. I used my right.

_____ **3.** He (bought/wanted) rice. I chose cheese.

_____ **4.** He was a son. I was a (girl/daughter).

_____ **5.** He had a nice cat. My dog sometimes was (naughty/bad).

_____ **6.** He found books about space. I (sought/had) books about animals.

_____ **7.** His mother (taught/did) math. My mom was an artist.

_____ **8.** What (brought/kept) us together? Being best friends!

Directions First, circle the words that have the vowel sound you hear in **ball**. Then match each circled word to its clue. Write each word on the line.

_____ **9.** a parent's female child

_____ **10.** what a boxer did

_____ **11.** paid for

_____ **12.** gave lessons

bought	**laughter**
found	**country**
fought	**taught**
could	**though**
daughter	

School + Home **Home Activity** This page practices words with the vowel sound in *ball* spelled *augh, ough*. Challenge your child to name two words that rhyme with *bought* and are spelled *ough* (*brought, thought*) and a word that rhymes with *caught* and is spelled *augh* (*taught*).

© Pearson Education C

Prefixes *over-, under-, out-*

Directions Add the prefix *over-, under-,* or *out-* to each base word.
Write the new word on the line.

1. over- + load   = _____

2. out-   + going = _____

3. under- + gone   = _____

4. over- + cooked = _____

5. out-   + field = _____

6. under- + paid   = _____

7. over- + due   = _____

8. out   + line   = _____

Directions Add the prefix *over-, under-,* or *out-* to the base word in ( )
to complete each sentence. Write the word on the line.

_____   9. When we lived in a hot country, I played (side) every day.

_____   10. My habits had to (go) a change when we moved to a place where it rained a lot.

_____   11. During the winter, I have to wear an (coat).

_____   12. I was (joyed) to find a friend who liked to play chess!

Home Activity This activity works with words with the prefixes *over-, under-,* and *out-*. Work together to list other words with these prefixes. Use a dictionary for ideas.

Name_____

Sequence

- The **sequence** of a story is the order in which events happen.
- **Clue words,** such as *first, next, then,* and *finally,* are often used to signal the sequence of events. Dates and times can also be clues. Sometimes, no clue words are used at all.

Directions Read the passage and use the information to complete the sequence chart below.

> My family came to this country so my great-grandfather could find land to farm. The first part of their trip was on a big ship. It took many weeks to sail across the sea. They landed in New York. Then they rode on a train. Finally, they loaded their things on a wagon pulled by a team of horses. They rode on the wagon to their new home in the Northwest. Grandmother showed me pictures of the house and the barns they put up. It's the same house we live in today. I have the same address as my great-grandfather!

Directions Circle the statements in the boxes that best tell the beginning, middle, and end of the family's journey to America.

Beginning
1. They rode on a big ship.
   They rode on a train.
   They looked for a farm.

Middle
2. They didn't like New York
   They rode on a train.
   They rode on a ship.

End
3. They rode on a wagon to the Northwest.
   They rode on a big ship.
   They rode on a train.

4. Circle clue words in the passage that tell the order of events. Then write them on the line below.

School + Home **Home Activity** The activity tells the order of events in a story. Find a short story. Read the story together and ask your child to tell what happened at the beginning, the middle, and the end of the story.

112 Comprehension Sequence

Practice Book Unit 5

© Pearson Education C

Name_____

Vocabulary

Directions Match each word with its definition. Write the word on the line.

_____ 1. a long trip

_____ 2. a picture taken with a camera

_____ 3. place where one lives

_____ 4. someone who comes to a country to live there

_____ 5. part of a large building where people live

_____ 6. where sets of objects are kept and displayed

Directions Write a word from the box to complete each sentence below.

7. Ann made the long _____ across the sea.

8. She was an _____ , and she wanted to live in a new country.

9. She was very happy to find an _____ for her family to live in.

10. She was proud to write her new _____ on letters to send back home.

Write a Story

Write a story about how an immigrant might feel about coming to America to live. Use as many vocabulary words as possible.

© Pearson Education C

School + Home **Home Activity** This page helps your child read and write vocabulary words. Ask your child to tell you about a journey, a museum, or a photograph. Encourage your child to use the vocabulary words.

Writing

Directions Circle the items you will use to draw a floor plan of an apartment.

markers	eraser	ink pen	paper
paste	pencils	photograph	ruler

Directions Decide the kind of apartment for which you will draw a floor plan. Put a checkmark beside your answers.

1. Whose apartment will you draw a floor plan for?

_____ a family of 1863 _____ a family of today

2. What rooms will be in the apartment?

_____ sitting room _____ kitchen

_____ bathroom _____ bedroom

_____ laundry room _____ dining room

_____ TV room _____ other rooms _____

3. How many rooms will be in the apartment?

_____ 3

_____ 4

_____ 5

_____ 6

_____ 7

On another sheet of paper, draw the floor plan of an apartment for a family you chose. Be sure to label each room.

Home Activity This page helps your child draw a floor plan for an apartment. Help your child make a list of the rooms in your house or apartment and draw a floor plan for your home. Encourage your child to add any rooms he or she would like to have. Help your child label the rooms.

© Pearson Education C

Name_____

Long *i: ind, ild;* Long *o: ost, old*

Directions Circle the words in the poem with the long *i* sound and underline the words with the long *o* sound. Write each word on the lines.

At the Market

At the market, what can you find?
Peppers of every kind.
Hot ones and mild ones.
Red, orange, and gold ones.
Fat ones and thin ones.
There's some wild-looking ones!
Sold fresh in the morning,
They're sauce by evening!

Peppers For Sale

Long *i* words

1. _____
2. _____
3. _____
4. _____

Long *o* words

5. _____
6. _____

Directions Choose the words from the box that rhyme with each of the words below. Write the words from the box on the lines.

7. kind _____ _____
8. wild _____ _____
9. sold _____ _____
10. most _____ _____

child	hold	told
host	mild	mind
grind	post	

Home Activity This page practices words with the long *i* sound as in *kind* and *child* and the long *o* sound as in *post* and *cold*. Challenge your child to name a single consonant that can be used to make words ending in *ind, ild, ost,* and *old*. (*mind, mild, most,* and *mold*)

© Pearson Education C

Name_____

Suffixes -y, -ish

Directions Add the suffix **-y** or **-ish** to each word. Write the new word on the line.

1. speed + y   = _____

2. snow + y   = _____

3. fool + ish = _____

4. child + ish = _____

5. meat + y   = _____

6. sleep + y   = _____

7. hand + y   = _____

8. yellow + ish = _____

9. boy + ish = _____

Directions Separate each base word from the suffix and write each part on the lines.

10. _____ + _____ = oily

11. _____ + _____ = childish

12. _____ + _____ = selfish

13. _____ + _____ = crusty

14. _____ + _____ = sticky

15. _____ + _____ = girlish

Home Activity This lesson uses base words and suffixes. Challenge your child to add suffixes to the base words *round, crunch, soap, green,* and *cloud* to make new words. (*roundish, crunchy, soapy, greenish,* and *cloudy*)

© Pearson Education C

Name_____

Draw Conclusions

- A **conclusion** is a decision or opinion that makes sense based on facts and details.
- You can also use **what you already know** to **draw a conclusion.**

Directions Read the passage and use the information to complete the chart below.

It's dinnertime, and I'm going to make French toast. I will try to make baked French toast. First, I'll put two thick slices of bread in milk and egg mixed together. Then, I'll put the soaked bread slices in a lightly greased baking pan. Next, I'll grind nutmeg for the top of each slice. And, finally, I'll bake it for 20 minutes. I'll serve it with butter and hot jam. It will make a great dinner.

Directions Answer the questions in boxes 1–4. Then write a conclusion about what you read.

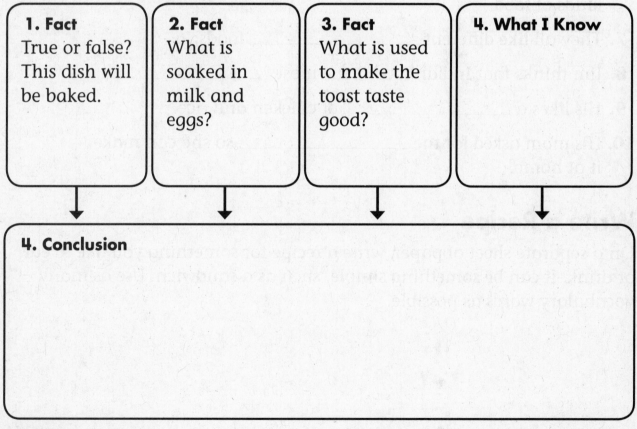

1. Fact	2. Fact	3. Fact	4. What I Know
True or false? This dish will be baked.	What is soaked in milk and eggs?	What is used to make the toast taste good?	

4. Conclusion

School + Home **Home Activity** This activity works with drawing conclusions. Have your child tell you about something that happened to him or her at school. Then help your child summarize what happened and draw a conclusion from it.

Vocabulary

Directions Match each word with its meaning. Draw a line to connect them.

1. delicious   a set of steps for cooking

2. ethnic   good to eat

3. recipe   a place to buy and eat a meal

4. restaurant   connected with a group of people

Check the Words You Know

__delicious
__dinnertime
__ethnic
__mixture
__recipe
__restaurant

Directions Write the word from the box that best completes each sentence below.

5. At _____ , my family likes to eat a big meal.

6. Jim's family likes to go to a _____ with many kinds of food.

7. They all like different _____ foods.

8. Jim thinks that Indian food is the most _____ .

9. His likes a _____ of chicken and rice.

10. His mom asked for the _____ so she can make it at home.

Write a Recipe

On a separate sheet of paper, write a recipe for something you like to eat or drink. It can be something simple, such as a sandwich. Use as many vocabulary words as possible.

© Pearson Education C

Home Activity This page helps your child read and write vocabulary words. Have your child plan a menu for dinner or help you prepare food from a written recipe. Encourage your child to use the vocabulary words in conversations.

Name_____

Writing

Directions Fill in the chart to create names for the items on a menu. Each word on a line should start with the same sound. The first one is done for you.

Person's Name	Adjective	Food
Tom's	**T**asty	**T**acos
		Dumplings
		Grapes
		Cake
		Soup
		Chicken

Directions Choose words from the following list to describe each dish. Circle the words you want to use.

chewy	delicious	select
chopped	golden	spicy
cold	great	stirred
cooked	green	sweet
dandy	simple	

Directions Make a list of other words you might use. Think about words that tell how the dish looks.

_____ _____

_____ _____

_____ _____

Home Activity This page helps your child write names and descriptions of foods. Work through the page with your child. Talk with your child about the foods that members of your family enjoy eating. Then help your child write another description of a favorite dish.

© Pearson Education C

Name_____

Syllables VCCCV

Directions Some words have three consonants in the middle, between two vowels: *monster, control.* Choose the word in ( ) with the VCCCV syllable pattern to finish each sentence. Write the word on the line.

_____ **1.** The (traveler, pilgrim) took a trip to another country.

_____ **2.** She went with a (hundred, thousand) other people.

_____ **3.** The food was different, but she didn't (complain, argue).

_____ **4.** She thinks that (holidays, surprises) are fun!

_____ **5.** She ate some dishes with lamb (instead, sometimes) of beef.

_____ **6.** She had a chance to (inspect, study) many old places.

Directions Circle the word in each group that has the VCCCV syllable pattern. Underline the letters that make the pattern.

7. human   partner   winner

8. constant   planet   signal

9. forgive   monster   wonder

10. complain   number   writer

11. beyond   robin   instant

12. chosen   control   copper

© Pearson Education C

Home Activity This page practices words with syllables that include VCCCV. Work through the items with your child. Write these words: *children, hundred, monster.* Ask your child to say the words and underline the VCCCV pattern.

Name_____

Main Idea and Supporting Details

- The **main idea** is what a story is all about.
- **Details** are small pieces of information that help tell what a story is about.
- As you read, **ask yourself,** "What are the important ideas in the story so far."
- **Sum up** to help you understand what is happening.

Directions Read the following story.

> **K**endra saw all sorts of colorful rocks at the beach. She had been looking for something to collect. Kendra decided she would collect rocks.
>
> Kendra loaded her backpack with red rocks and speckled rocks.
>
> At home, Kendra looked for a place to keep her rocks. She found a pretty box. She put the rocks in the box and set it on the porch.
>
> Kendra showed her rocks to everyone who came to visit.

Directions Complete the graphic organizer to tell what the story is all about.

Supporting Details

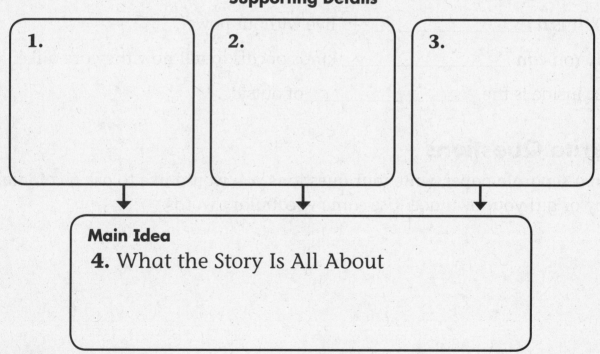

1.

2.

3.

Main Idea

4. What the Story Is All About

School + Home **Home Activity** This page allows your child to find the main idea of a story. Work through the items with your child. Read a story with your child. Ask him or her to tell the main idea—what the story is all about.

Name_____

Vocabulary

Directions Draw a line from the word to its definition.

1. compare   to make or become better

2. hardship   as different as it can be

3. improve   to tell how things are alike

4. opposite   to set up a home in a new country or place

5. settle

6. surround   something hard to put up with

    to shut in on all sides; enclose

> **Check the Words You Know**
>
> __compare
> __hardship
> __improve
> __opposite
> __settle
> __surround

Directions Fill in the blank with a word from the box that fits the meaning of the sentence.

7. He built a fence to _____ the horses.

8. Reading books helps you _____ your skills.

9. Some people decided to _____ in the West.

10. It is a _____ to live without power.

11. You can _____ kinds of cats to tell how they are alike.

12. Inside is the _____ of outside.

Write Questions

On a separate paper, write four questions you would like to ask a colonial boy or girl your own age. Use some vocabulary words.

Home Activity This page helps your child read and write vocabulary words. Work through the items with your child. Ask your child to tell two ways his or her life is different from that of a colonial child.

© Pearson Education C

Name_____

Writing

Think about times in the past—even millions of years ago when there were dinosaurs! Choose a time.

Directions Circle any words from the box that you might use in your writing. Now answer these questions.

thrilling	games
creepy	food
hardship	school
power	chores
plumbing	boring
toys	

1. What time in the past did you choose?

_____

2. What are some of your favorite things to do?

_____

_____

3. Could you do these things in the past? Explain.

_____

_____

4. What could you do in the past that you can't do now?

_____

_____

5. What would be hard if you lived in the past? What would be fun?

_____

_____

On another paper, write a paragraph telling if you would or would not like to live in the past. Explain your reasons.

School + Home **Home Activity** This page helps your child write sentences about a topic. Work through the page with your child. Then have your child read the paragraph aloud.

Name _____

Suffixes -hood, -ment

Directions Combine the base word and the suffix. Write the new word on the line.

1. pay   +   -ment = _____

2. boy   +   -hood = _____

3. excite   +   -ment = _____

4. agree   +   -ment = _____

5. child   +   -hood = _____

6. move   +   -ment = _____

7. false   +   -hood = _____

8. neighbor +   -hood = _____

Directions Add **-hood** or **-ment** to the base word in ( ) to complete each sentence. Use the word box for help. Write the new word on the line.

_____

9. The baby's (enjoy) of the toy made us smile.

_____

10. Mrs. Brown enjoys (mother).

_____

11. The puppy grew fast with the good (treat).

_____

12. I was filled with (amaze) when I saw a rainbow.

amazement
treatment
enjoyment
motherhood

© Pearson Education C

School + Home **Home Activity** This page practices words with the suffixes *-hood* and *-ment*. Work through the items with your child. Ask your child to name three things that cause him or her excitement.

124 **Phonics** Suffixes *-hood, -ment*

Practice Book Unit 6

Name _____

Prefixes pre-, mid-, post-

Directions Add the prefix **pre-**, **mid-**, or **post-** to each base word. Write the new word on the line.

1. mid- + point = _____

2. pre- + heat = _____

3. post- + war = _____

4. mid- + way = _____

5. mid- + west = _____

6. pre- + teen = _____

7. post- + date = _____

8. pre- + view = _____

Directions Choose the word from the box that best fits the definition. Write the word on the line.

_____ **9.** to cook something before

_____ **10.** the middle of the week

_____ **11.** to pay ahead of time

_____ **12.** the middle of the day

midday
midweek
precook
prepay

© Pearson Education C

Home Activity This page practices words with the prefixes *pre-*, *mid-*, and *post-*. Work through the items with your child. Ask your child to name a month in midsummer and to tell what time it is at midnight.

Name _____

Main Idea

- The **main idea** is what a passage is all about.
- **Details** are small pieces of information that tell about the main idea.

Directions Read the passage. Then answer the questions below.

> Long ago, people came to the United States from other countries. They came through Ellis Island. It is about a mile outside of New York City. It is named after Samuel Ellis who owned the island. He sold it to the state of New York.
>
> About 22 million people came through Ellis Island. They were given medical exams. A wall at Ellis Island has some of the people's names written on it. There is a Web site that has a list of people who came through Ellis Island.

1. What is the passage about?

_____

Give four details about Ellis Island.

2. _____

3. _____

4. _____

5. _____

6. Is the passage fiction or nonfiction? How do you know?

_____

_____

_____

_____

School + Home **Home Activity** This page helps your child identify the main idea and details in a passage. Work through the items with your child. Talk with your child about people coming to the United States from other countries.

Name _____

Vocabulary

Directions Fill in the word from the box that fits the meaning of the sentence.

1. An elephant is an _____ animal.

2. A heart is a _____ for love.

3. The statue in the town square is a _____ to soldiers.

4. The soldiers fought for our country's _____ .

5. A _____ carved the monument out of stone.

6. There is a statue of _____ Abraham Lincoln in Washington, D.C.

Directions Draw a line from the word to its definition.

7. enormous   the leader of a country

8. liberty   freedom

9. monument   a person who carves or models figures

10. president   something set up to honor a person or an event

11. sculptor   something that stands for or represents something else

12. symbol   very, very large; huge

Write a Letter

On a separate paper, write a letter to the president of the United States. Write at least three sentences. Use as many of the vocabulary words as you can.

School + Home

Home Activity This page helps your child read and write vocabulary words. Work through the items with your child. Then have your child tell what the vocabulary words in his or her letter mean.

© Pearson Education C

Name _____

Writing

- A **chart** can help you organize your ideas.

Directions Fill in the right side of the chart to tell about your school.

My School

Questions	Answers
What is the name of your school?	
Is the school named after a famous person? Who?	
What are the school colors?	
What is special about the school?	

Make a flag for your school. Answer these questions.

1. What shape will your flag be? _____

2. What colors will you use? _____

3. What people will you show? _____

4. What animals will you show? _____

On another paper, draw your flag. Write sentences to tell what the colors and symbols mean. Make sure your words are spelled correctly.

Home Activity This page helps your child design and describe a flag. Work through the page with your child. Then have your child read the description aloud.

© Pearson Education C

Name _____

Syllables V/V

Directions Circle the word with two vowels together that make two different sounds. Then underline the letters that stand for the two different sounds.

1. clean   paint   patio

2. media   faith   search

3. greed   journal   rodeo

4. either   cruel   southern

5. beach   pound   pioneer

6. diet   poison   waiter

7. grain   group   stadium

8. ago   freeze   areas

Directions Read the paragraph. Circle the underlined words that have two vowels together that make two different sounds. Write the words on the lines.

Meg was eager to create a new song. She thought she had an idea for a tune. She tried it on the piano. Then she wrote a part for the violin. She liked the way it sounded.

Meg invited two friends to go to the studio with her. Her friends were singers. Meg explained the music. The trio made a recording. Someday you might even hear it on the radio.

9. _____   13. _____

10. _____   14. _____

11. _____   15. _____

12. _____

© Pearson Education C

School + Home **Home Activity** This page practices words with syllables V/V. Work through the items with your child. Ask your child to read aloud the words he or she wrote on the page.

Name _____

Sequence

- **Sequence** is the order in which things happen in a story.
- **Clue words,** such as *before* and *after*, can tell you when something happens.

Directions Read the story. Then answer the questions below.

One morning, two bears woke up. They were hungry. The day before, they had eaten all the berries on their side of the river. "Look at those berries on the other side of the river," said Grizzly Bear. "If we jump up when the wind blows, we can catch a ride to our dinner."

Just then, a strong wind came up. The bears jumped into the air and were carried across the river. They landed among hundreds of berries. The bears ate enough to fill their bellies. After that, they felt sleepy. They took a long nap.

1. How did the bears feel when they first woke up?

_____

2. What idea did Grizzly Bear have for getting food?

_____

_____

3. What happened after Grizzly Bear told the other bear his idea?

_____

_____

4. How did the bears feel after they filled their bellies?

_____

5. What did the bears do last?

_____

6. What clue words did you find in the story?

_____

Home Activity This page helps your child identify the sequence of events in a story. Work through the items with your child. Read another story about animals with your child. Ask your child to tell what happened first, next, and last.

Name _____

Vocabulary

Directions Choose the word from the box that matches each definition. Write the word on the line.

Check the Words You Know

__adopt
__capture
__comfort
__exercise
__provide
__struggle

_____ **1.** to make prisoner of; take by force

_____ **2.** to give what is needed or wanted; supply

_____ **3.** to make great efforts with the body; try hard

_____ **4.** to take for your own or as your own choice

_____ **5.** ease; freedom from hardship

_____ **6.** the active use of the body or mind for its improvement

Directions Circle the word at the end of each sentence that fits the meaning. Then write the word on the line to finish the sentence.

7. If you want a kitten, you can _____ one from the animal shelter.   adopt   give

8. Animals need _____ to stay healthy.   clothes   exercise

9. A rabbit will _____ if you pick it up. It doesn't like to be held.   struggle   bark

10. Food, water, and a place to live give most animals _____ . sadness   comfort

Write Sentences

On a separate paper, write three things wild horses need. Use complete sentences. Use as many vocabulary words as you can.

School + Home

Home Activity This page helps your child read and write vocabulary words. Work through the items with your child. Ask your child to tell you why a wild horse would *not* make a good pet.

© Pearson Education C

Name _____

Writing

Think about the wild animals in your neighborhood. Think about what can help them and hurt them. You will make a poster to tell other people.

Directions Circle any words from the box that you might use. Write other words you can use on your poster.

healthy
safe
happy
hurt
free
wild

1. _____

Now answer the questions.

2. What wild animals live near you?

_____

_____

3. Do you think people should feed wild animals? Why or why not?

_____

_____

4. If someone puts poison in a garden to kill insects, what could happen to wild animals?

_____

_____

5. If people leave trash, broken bottles, and old furniture outside, what could happen to wild animals?

_____

_____

Tape four papers together so you have a big poster. Write a title for your poster. List things people should and should not do to keep wild animals safe. You can draw pictures or paste pictures from magazines.

School + Home **Home Activity** This page helps your child make a poster. Work through the page with your child. Have your child read the poster aloud.

© Pearson Education C

Name _____

Common Syllables

Directions Read the passage. Circle each word that ends in **-tion,** **-sion,** or **-ture.** Then write each word in the correct column.

Summer vacation was filled with excitement. One day we went to see the sculpture garden in the park. Another time we watched some artists as they painted a giant mural. Each division of the mural showed a different time in our country's history. The last part showed the artist's vision for the future of our nation.

-tion	-sion	-ture
1. _____	3. _____	5. _____
2. _____	4. _____	6. _____

Directions Choose the word from the box that finishes each word below. Two letters in each word are given. Write the other letters to complete the word.

7. __ __ r __ __ t __ __ __

8. f __ __ __ __ __ e

9. __ __ s s __ __ __

10. __ c t __ __ __

11. __ x __ __ __ s __ __ __ __ __

12. __ r __ __ __ __ __ e

13. __ __ __ n __ __ __ __ e

14. i __ __ __ __ __ __ __ t __ __ __

15. __ __ n s __ __ __

action
creature
direction
expression
feature
furniture
imagination
mansion
mission

Home Activity This page practices words with the syllables *-tion, -sion,* and *-ture.* Work through the items with your child. Ask your child to write one sentence with the word *picture* and one with the word *question.*

© Pearson Education C

Multisyllabic Word Practice

Directions Underline the word in each sentence that has **three** syllables or parts. Then write the word on the line. Draw lines to divide the word into parts (example: un|der|line).

_____ 1. I have a lot of furniture in my room: a bed, desk, chair, lamp, rug, and bookcase.

_____ 2. The roaring lion had a scary expression on its face.

_____ 3. The audience laughed when the actor fell off his chair.

_____ 4. A clown will entertain the children at the birthday party.

_____ 5. The last performance of the movie is at nine o'clock.

_____ 6. A parade on Independence Day is a tradition in our town.

_____ 7. I must remember to study for the science test on Friday.

_____ 8. The city looked beautiful after the big snowfall.

Directions Underline the word in each sentence that has **four** syllables and write the word on the line. Draw lines to divide the word into parts.

_____ 9. In our community, people help their neighbors.

_____ 10. The judges made presentations for the prize cows at the fair.

© Pearson Education C

School + Home **Home Activity** This page practices words with three and four syllables. Work through the items with your child. Ask your child to say two sentences: one with the word *important* and one with the word *tomorrow*.

Name _____

Compare and Contrast

- When you **compare and contrast,** you tell how things are alike and different.

- Look for **clue words** that signal comparisons and contrasts, such as *like, both, different,* and *however.*

- As you read, **ask yourself,** "How are these things alike? How are they different? What do I already know about these things?"

Directions Read the passage. Then answer the questions below.

Two big rivers in the world are the Nile and the Amazon. Both rivers are very long. However, the Amazon has more water flowing in it.

The Nile and the Amazon differ in another way. They are on two different continents. The Nile is in Africa. The Amazon is in South America.

There are many animals in both rivers. Crocodiles live in both the Amazon and the Nile. Unlike the Nile, the Amazon is home to one of the world's longest snakes, the anaconda.

1. What is one way the Amazon and Nile Rivers are alike?

_____

2. Are the Amazon and Nile located on different continents? What are the continents?

_____

3. What animal is found in the Amazon but not in the Nile?

_____

4. What is one animal that the Nile and Amazon have in common?

_____

5. How else might the Amazon and Nile rivers be alike?

_____

© Pearson Education C

 Home Activity This page helps your child compare and contrast. Work through the items with your child. Choose two things in your home, such as a table and a desk or a cat and a dog. Ask your child to tell how they are alike and different.

Name _____

Vocabulary

Directions Choose the word from the box that matches each definition. Write the word on the line.

1. a way to show things _____

2. to fill with a thought or feeling _____

3. to cause to laugh or smile _____

4. a place where plays are acted _____

5. to make a thing that has not been made before; cause to be _____

6. to put into words _____

> **Check the Words You Know**
>
> __amuse
> __create
> __display
> __express
> __inspire
> __theater

Directions Fill in the blank with a word from the box that fits the meaning of the sentence.

7. There is a _____ of students' artwork in the hall.

8. Does the picture of a pig wearing a dress _____ you?

9. Sam likes to _____ pictures by pasting bottle tops on cardboard.

10. Artists _____ their ideas in many different ways.

11. I like the posters that are outside the movie _____ .

12. Sometimes they _____ me to see a certain movie.

Write an Ad

On a separate paper, write an ad for Pete's apple market. Make his apples sound yummy. Use as many of the vocabulary words as you can.

© Pearson Education C

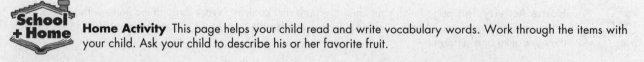

Home Activity This page helps your child read and write vocabulary words. Work through the items with your child. Ask your child to describe his or her favorite fruit.

Name _____

Writing

Think about different ways to express yourself: art, acting, singing, dancing, writing.
Think about how to describe the form of expression.

create	words
pretend	imagination
movement	express
draw	exciting
paint	thrilling

1. What way to express yourself is your favorite?

_____

2. What do you like best about it?

_____

3. How does it make you feel?

_____

4. Do you like other people to watch as you do it or to look at it when it is
finished? Why or why not?

_____

_____

5. Write a good sentence to begin your description.

_____

On another paper, write your description. You can use words from the box
to help you. Make sure all your words are spelled correctly.

School + Home **Home Activity** This page helps your child write a description. Work through the page with your child. Then
have your child read the description aloud.

Name _____

Blending Multisyllabic Words

Directions Each word below has one or more word parts added to the beginning or the end of its base word. Underline the base word. Then write a sentence that uses the whole word.

1. unreasonable _____

2. carefully _____

3. disagreement _____

4. reappeared _____

5. unprepared _____

6. endlessly _____

Directions Each base word below has a word part added to the beginning and end. Separate each base word from the other word parts and write each part on a line.

Base Word

7. _____ + _____ + _____ = distasteful

8. _____ + _____ + _____ = unfriendly

9. _____ + _____ + _____ = unplugged

10. _____ + _____ + _____ = unhappily

11. _____ + _____ + _____ = unlawful

12. _____ + _____ + _____ = dishonestly

13. _____ + _____ + _____ = renewable

14. _____ + _____ + _____ = refreshment

15. _____ + _____ + _____ = distrustful

© Pearson Education C

School + Home **Home Activity** This page practices words with prefixes and suffixes. Work through the items with your child. Ask your child how the base word *easy* changes when the suffix *-ly* is added.

Name _____

Main Idea

- The **main idea** is the most important idea in a passage. It tells what the passage is about.
- **Supporting details** are small pieces of information that tell about the main idea.

Some animals are born in unusual ways.

A frog begins as an egg. The egg hatches in about a week, and a small tadpole wiggles out. A tadpole looks a bit like a tiny fish. It swims around in water, looking for food to eat. As the tadpole eats, it grows and changes. It loses its tail and grows legs. Soon the tadpole is a frog.

A butterfly begins as an egg too. The egg hatches in a month, and out comes a caterpillar. A hard shell grows around the caterpillar. Inside the shell, the animal changes again. In about three weeks, out flies a butterfly!

Directions Read the passage. Then answer the questions below.

1. What is the main idea of the passage?

_____

2. Give three details about a frog.

_____

_____

_____

3. Give three details about a butterfly.

_____

_____

_____

© Pearson Education C

School + Home   **Home Activity** This page helps your child identify the main idea and details in a passage. Work through the items with your child. Read a story with your child. Then ask your child to tell the main idea of the story.

Name _____

Vocabulary

Directions Circle the word that completes each sentence. Then write the word on the line.

Check the Words You Know		
_annoy	_disturb	_pollution
_cooperate	_intention	_require

1. Please be quiet and don't _____ me when I am studying.

   disturb   cooperate

2. The oil spill caused _____ in the ocean.

   intention   pollution

3. If we _____ and work together, we can finish our project sooner.

   cooperate   annoy

4. Mosquito bites _____ me—they itch!

   require   annoy

Directions Choose a word from the box that matches each definition. Write the word on the line.

5. actions that make the environment dirty _____

6. to work together _____

7. to need _____

8. a purpose; plan _____

Write Laws

Write three silly laws. Write one law about pigs, one law about roller skating, and one law about hot dogs. Use as many of the vocabulary words as you can.

© Pearson Education C

School + Home **Home Activity** This page helps your child read and write vocabulary words. Work through the items with your child. Make up a silly law for your child to follow. Ask him or her to make up a silly law for you to follow.

Name _____

Writing

Think about what would make the world a better place. Think about what would make life more fun. Look at the words and phrases in the box for ideas.

1. What are three problems in the world that make you sad?

food	school
home	bedtime
healthy	pet
happy	television

_____

_____

_____

2. How could someone fix those things?

_____

_____

_____

3. What are three things you would *really* like to do or have?

_____

_____

_____

On another paper, write a law. For example, all children must have enough food to eat. Make sure all the words in your law are spelled correctly.

© Pearson Education C

Home Activity This page helps your child write a law. Work through the page with your child. Ask your child if being the person to fix a problem would be a hard job or an easy job and tell why.

Related Words

Directions Choose the word that best matches each clue. Write the word on the line.

1. coverings for the body   cloth   clothes   _____

2. a person who plays sports   athlete   athletic   _____

3. a person's handwritten name   sign   signature   _____

4. water in a tub for washing   bath   bathe   _____

5. the world of living things
   and the outdoors   natural   nature   _____

Directions The two related words in ( ) are missing from each sentence. Write the words in the correct places to complete each sentence.

6. The _____ writes _____ that rhymes.
   (poet, poetry)

7. To _____ a word means to give its _____ .
   (define, definition)

8. Hot _____ ash came out of the _____ .
   (volcano, volcanic)

9. The _____ weather _____ the campers.
   (pleased, pleasant)

10. I will _____ what _____ to make after I
    have heard all the facts. (decide, decision)

11. I enjoyed the _____ because the _____
    were very good actors. (performers, performance)

12. To avoid _____ , don't _____ yourself.
    (repeat, repetition)

Home Activity This page practices related words. Work through the items with your child. Ask your child to say or write a sentence that uses the words *please* (or *pleased*) and *pleasant*.

© Pearson Education C

Name_____

Draw Conclusions

- A **conclusion** is a decision you reach based on what you read and what you know.
- Use **facts** and **details** to help you reach a conclusion.

Directions Read the passage. Then complete the chart below.

Sandy heard about the whales, so she hurried down to the bay. It was in the middle of a winter blizzard. Instead of swimming out to sea, whales had gone through the channel. Now the whales were stuck in ice.

People were helping the whales. Sandy helped chip ice to free them.

Firefighters brought hoses and other supplies. The tide was rising. Everyone waited to see what would happen.

The swish of water from the hoses sounded like a symphony. The water melted the ice. The whales wiggled loose.

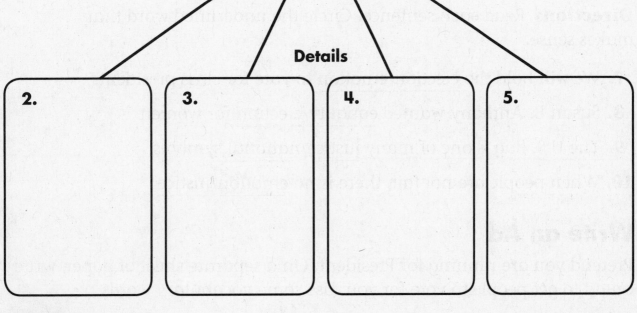

1. Conclusion: What do you think happened to the whales?

Details

2.

3.

4.

5.

© Pearson Education C

Home Activity This page helps your child practice drawing conclusions. Work through the items with your child. Read part of a new story with your child. Stop and ask your child to draw a conclusion about the story.

Name_____

Vocabulary

Directions Solve each riddle using a word from the box. Write the word on the line.

1. I am a strong feeling.

   What am I? _____

2. I am another word for say.

   What am I? _____

3. I describe something that belongs to a nation.

   What am I? _____

4. I am another word for fairness.

   What am I? _____

5. I am a word for how things are equal.

   What am I? _____

6. I am an act of choosing by voting.

   What am I? _____

Directions Read each sentence. Circle the underlined word that makes sense.

7. We will hold the election/emotion to vote for class president.

8. Susan B. Anthony wanted equality/election for women.

9. The U.S. flag is one of many justice/national symbols.

10. When people are not fair, there is no emotion/justice.

Write an Ad

Pretend you are running for President. On a separate sheet of paper, write an ad to get people to vote for you. Use some vocabulary words.

Home Activity This page helps your child read and write vocabulary words. Work through the items with your child. Ask your child to read his or her ad to you.

© Pearson Education C

Name_____

Writing

Directions Sometimes it can be difficult to hold on to our freedom. Read each question. Write your answers on the lines.

1. How did Susan B. Anthony feel about voting?

_____

_____

2. What did Susan B. Anthony do to help women vote?

_____

_____

3. How did Androcles feel about both equality and freedom?

_____

_____

4. Why was Androcles set free?

_____

_____

5. What things can you vote on at school?

_____

_____

On another paper, tell about one way people hold on to freedom. Tell why it is important. Use some vocabulary words. Check your spelling.

© Pearson Education C

Home Activity This page helps your child write about freedom. Work through the page with your child. Then ask your child to tell how to hold on to freedom.

Name _____

Words for Writing and Reading

_____   _____

_____   _____

_____   _____

_____   _____

_____   _____

_____   _____

_____   _____

_____   _____

_____   _____

_____   _____

_____   _____

_____   _____

_____   _____

_____   _____

_____   _____

_____   _____

_____   _____

Name _____

Words for Writing and Reading

_____   _____
_____   _____
_____   _____
_____   _____
_____   _____
_____   _____
_____   _____
_____   _____
_____   _____
_____   _____
_____   _____
_____   _____
_____   _____
_____   _____
_____   _____
_____   _____

Name _____

Reading Log

Date	What is the title?	Who is the author?	What did you think of it?

Name _____

Reading Log

Date	What is the title?	Who is the author?	What did you think of it?

Name _____

Reading Log

Date	What is the title?	Who is the author?	What did you think of it?

Name _____

Reading Log

Date	What is the title?	Who is the author?	What did you think of it?

Name _____

Reading Log

Date	What is the title?	Who is the author?	What did you think of it?